TALES FROM THE P.

CH00704453

A hundred years of parish councils in East Sussex

LOCAL GOVERNMENT ACT, 1894.

The reverend Clement Powell
Newick

You are hereby summoned to attend the FIRST MEETING of the COUNCIL for the Parish of _Newick_ to be held at _The National School for Boys_ at _eight_ o'clock p.m. on _Thursday 3rd January 1895_ when the following business will be transacted :—

    1. To take Declaration of Acceptance of Office.

    2. To elect a Chairman.

    3. To elect a Vice-Chairman, if desired.

    4. To appoint a Treasurer, if desired

    5. To appoint a Clerk and assign his salary, if any.

    6. To transact necessary and immediate business in connection with the transfer of books from the Overseers, Churchwardens, Vestry, or any other Authority, and to receive and provide for the custody of all parish books and documents, the custody of which is, by the Local Government Act, transferred to the Parish Council.

Dated this _21st_ day of December, 1894.

Thomas Baden Powell, _Chairman._

Printed and Published by FARNCOMBE & Co., "East Sussex News" Office, Lewes.

David Arscott

S.B. Publications

By the same author:

The Sussex Story
Curiosities of East Sussex
Curiosities of West Sussex
Hastings and the 1066 Country
Philip's County Guide: West Sussex (general editor)
A Sussex Quiz Book
The Upstart Gardener
Explore Sussex
Agelines

(with Warden Swinfen):

Hidden Sussex
People of Hidden Sussex
Hidden Sussex Day by Day
Hidden Sussex — the Towns

Video narration:

Discovering Brighton
Discovering West Sussex

Front cover: *The parish pump at Newick*
Back cover: *Barcombe village*
(from postcard collections owned by the two parish councils)
Title page: *A summons to the rector of Newick to attend the first meeting of the parish council. The Rev Clement Powell, whose sprawling sermons regularly ran for 45 minutes, compiled a Newick hymn book and wrote new tunes for several of the old hymns*

First published in 1994 by S.B. Publications
in association with the Sussex Association of Local Councils,
c/o 19 Grove Road, Seaford, East Sussex BN25 1TP

© Copyright 1994 David Arscott

ISBN: 1.85770.057.0

Typeset and printed by Island Press Ltd, 0323 490222, UK

CONTENTS

ACKNOWLEDGEMENTS

Tales from the Parish Pump was commissioned by the Sussex Association of Local Councils with generous support from East Sussex County Council. The author would like to thank the many people who contributed to his researches, among them those hard-pressed parish clerks and chairmen who responded to his detailed questionnaire.

Documents from the archives are reproduced by kind permission of the local councils concerned and of the East Sussex County Council Record Office at Lewes, whose staff were unfailingly helpful and friendly. Further thanks to various individuals who supplied illustrative material: Alan Cannings, Doris Hall, Herbert Newbery, Lesley Scammell, Kathleen Verrall, David Wilkins and Doris Williams.

The parish council minutes reproduced in 'The Parishes at War' and 'Dad's Army Days' have been given standardised spelling, punctuation and style, and have undergone a small amount of silent editing to remove unwanted names and other material.

THE CENTENARY 101

The parish councils, parish meetings and town councils of East Sussex have equal status under the law, although the range of their activities obviously varies enormously. There were 101 of these local councils in 1994, all of them parish councils save the ones marked PM (parish meeting) or TC (town council).

Alciston (PM)
Alfriston
Arlington
Ashburnham & Penhurst
Barcombe
Battle (TC)
Beckley
Beddingham with Glynde
Berwick
Bodiam
Brede
Brightling
Burwash
Buxted
Camber
Catsfield
Chailey
Chalvington & Ripe
Chiddingly
Crowborough (TC)
Crowhurst
Cuckmere Valley
Dallington
Danehurst
Ditchling
East Chiltington
East Dean & Friston
East Guldeford (PM)
East Hoathly
Etchingham
Ewhurst
Fairlight
Falmer
Firle

Fletching
Forest Row
Framfield
Frant
Guestling
Hadlow Down
Hailsham (TC)
Hamsey
Hartfield
Heathfield & Waldron
Hellingly
Herstmonceux
Hooe
Horam
Hurst Green
Icklesham
Iden
Iford (PM)
Isfield
Kingston
Laughton
Lewes (TC)
Little Horsted (PM)
Long Man
Maresfield
Mayfield
Mountfield
Newhaven (TC)
Newick
Ninfield
Northiam
Peacehaven (TC)
Peasemarsh
Pett

Pevensey
Piddinghoe
Playden
Plumpton
Polegate (TC)
Ringmer
Rodmell
Rotherfield
Rye (TC)
Rye Foreign
Salehurst
Sedlescombe
Selmeston (PM)
South Heighton
Southease (PM)
St Ann (Without), Lewes (PM)
St John (Without), Lewes (PM)
Streat (PM)
Tarring Neville (PM)
Telscombe (TC)
Ticehurst
Uckfield (TC)
Udimore
Wadhurst
Warbleton
Wartling
Westfield
Westham
Westmeston
Whatlington
Willingdon & Jevington
Withyham
Wivelsfield

PROLOGUE

The village has a seemingly unassailable place in the English dream as a place of quiet retreat, with cricket on the green, church bells chiming over the pond, plump fruit ready for picking along the hedgerows and any number of similarly comforting images, all of them totally resistant to brute reality. Although parish councils are inevitably touched and warmed by this rural glow (one picture we have of the clerk may be of an unworldly, endearingly short-sighted, little body perambulating his or her narrow bounds of post office, general stores and vestry with a fistful of papers for the noticeboard), they nevertheless generate quite another, far less winsome, set of stock responses.

Since this book sets out to sketch the story of the parishes in their first hundred years, we had better confront those less than flattering prejudices at the outset. Is there not, for instance, something irredeemably comic in the notion of an earnest huddle of (predominantly middle class) men and women tirelessly discussing, say, the siting of a lamppost or the provision of a litter bin? There is, after all, a far bigger world outside, where war, famine and disease cry out for urgent attention.

Are these councils, moreover, not niggling mini bureaucracies, delighting in the creation of paperwork, their justification the passing of tedious minutes (in both senses of the phrase) at ill-attended meetings in draughty halls? Are they not irrelevant, in an age when our horizons have broadened far beyond the place where we park our car and sleep the night? And — perhaps the most damning criticism of all — are they not simply ineffectual, genuine political power being exercised well above their pathetic parochial heads?

All true, to a point — yet these apparently devastating salvoes surely miss the mark. The value of our parish councils (and of the town councils which, having the same powers, are also included in this centenary celebration) lies precisely in their self-evident narrowness of vision. Your lampposts and litter bins, your playgrounds and roadside verges, may mean nothing to me, but those in my own community contribute, in however small a way, to my overall quality of life. They are, to be bolshie about it, nobody else's business. And if, ultimately, my own local council has no power to prevent an unwanted road or housing development sanctioned by a higher authority, it can at least inform and agitate on behalf of its small, beleaguered population. Who else will do the job?

The grandest claim on behalf of the parishes — that they represent democracy at its most basic level — has to be entered with reservations. Few of us trouble ourselves with the bread-and-butter business of local affairs, and it is a diligent parish council which weighs the demands of a clamorous pressure group against what may be the very different desire of the silent majority.

That, however, is the perennial challenge of democracy, locally as much as nationally: whether through action or inaction, we get the services we deserve. Although the parish councils enter their second century in the comforting knowledge that they alone among the existing three tiers of local government are sure to survive an imminent reorganisation (perhaps, indeed, with their powers slightly increased), this should be a cause less for smugness than for determination. While recognising the many past achievements of our parish councils, we should remind ourselves that their future effectiveness depends, very largely, on us.

DAVID ARSCOTT

MR GLADSTONE'S PEASANT UPRISING

Did Henry Lane, in his fancy, hear the ghastly swish of Madame Guillotine that winter's night as he closed the door of his rural mansion behind him and set out in the darkness for Westmeston school?

It was Tuesday December 4, 1894. Throughout the land the common people were on the move, armed with a new and revolutionary weapon which might change the balance of power in the countryside for ever.

Mr Gladstone, the great Liberal leader, had at last had his way. The democratic spirit which had been steadily extending the franchise had now produced an Act of Parliament which would, he claimed, 'carry home to the minds of the peasants and the agricultural labourers the principles and the obligations, and . . . secure fully to them the benefits, of local government.'

Under this new legislation (which also created urban and rural district councils) each parish was to hold an annual meeting at which, in effect, every resident was entitled to vote. Those with three hundred or more inhabitants must elect a parish council, while those with more than a hundred on the roll could choose to do so. Not only were women included on the register of electors, but they could stand as councillors, too.

As the local squire, having inherited most of Streat and Westmeston, Lane was well aware that a suffering countryside was sinking into an ever deeper recession. Wheat prices had just fallen to their lowest level for a century. Depressed conditions had some years previously brought assertive farm workers together to form the Kent and Sussex Labourers Union: would this wretched legislation not give the men ideas well above their station?

For weeks on end the new Act had been discussed in public halls, in the pulpit and in the press — and, despite pious hopes from both sides, had divided many parishes along party political lines. Lord Brassey, the Liberal MP for Hastings, had hitherto ruled Catsfield from his French-style chateau, Normanhurst Court. He surrendered his position with good grace.

'It is no longer possible,' Brassey told his assembled villagers, 'that all that concerns the parish is to be dealt with by a few privileged individuals. Normanhurst and places like this are no longer to be places of government. We have, from the house which I have the fortune to occupy, been able to do a few good things for our neighbours, but we are not to *govern* our neighbourhood from Normanhurst.'

Change had been a long time coming. True, the parishes had always been used for civil as well as for ecclesiastical purposes — organising rudimentary policing, overseeing road repairs, even (until the Poor Law Amendment Act of 1834) administering the poor law — but the system was by now creaking uncomfortably. Not only had a confusion of authorities sprung up in town and countryside (among them sanitary boards and the poor law unions,

Vestry days. Before Gladstone's 1894 Act brought democracy to the countryside, the bailiff of the largest estate in a village would often double as parish clerk. Our picture shows a former clerk of Westmeston, Henry Edwards, carrying his staff of office — a short ebony cane with silver top.

whose territory included groups of neighbouring parishes), but the church continued to play an anachronistic, patently un-democratic, ringmaster's role.

Before Gladstone's legislation, the affairs of each parish were controlled by a small clique of the wealthy and influential which nominated an overseer and his salaried assistants at so-called vestry meetings under the chairmanship of the vicar — though the austere confines of the church room were very often abandoned for more comfortable quarters, among them the Bull at Ditchling, the Royal Oak at Whatlington and the Yew Tree beer house at Arlington.

This cosy arrangement was about to end, and not only in the sense that all parish meetings were, by law, to be held in non-licensed premises. The church would soon be reduced to looking after its own affairs, with the new civil authorities managing theirs. Allotments, burial grounds, cottage sanitation, libraries, footpaths: matters such as these were to be administered *by* the people *for* the people. Professional assessors and collectors of rates would no doubt keep their jobs, and the first wave of parish clerks would be drawn from the ranks of the assistant overseers (although it is interesting to note a letter to the *Sussex Express*, claiming that such men were 'often comparatively illiterate' and arguing the case for schoolmasters and postmasters to take on the job). In every other respect, however, there would be refreshing change. Had not the president of the National Liberal Association, calling the legislation 'the Charter of the peasants' liberty', promised that it would 'abolish patronage and banish privilege'?

In the light of such claims it is not surprising to sense, as December 4 approached, some ill-disguised alarm in the pronouncements of those who stood to lose power under the new arrangements. The Bishop of Chichester, addressing a diocesan conference at Lewes town hall, insisted that 'the landowner, the clergyman, the farmer and the tradesman must not hold aloof from the parish council.'

His fear was obvious: that well-organised helots would seize control of the councils for themselves.

'I trust,' the bishop went on, 'that there will be none of that unhappy abstention which is so mischievous in France and in the United States and perhaps, in our local and municipal elections, not unknown among ourselves, and which induces the upper classes, the natural leaders of the people, to desert their posts, leaving the field open to designing demagogues and to all the evils of party spirit and jobbery.

'I also have great confidence in the solid, sober sense, moderation and good feeling of the Sussex

Lewes town hall, where the Bishop of Chichester, the Right Rev Bishop Tuffnell, urged 'the natural leaders of the people' to prevent 'designing demagogues' from seizing control of the new parish councils.

agricultural labourer, and I do not doubt that he will be a most useful element in the parish councils.'

Since he went on to urge these honest citizens 'to use their influence on the side of peace and of equity', it is clear that he feared the very opposite. He was not alone in this.

Villagers at Maresfield, where the rector was unsympathetic to the new Act, were given a no-nonsense talk by G. F. Chambers, the author of an explanatory book on the subject. Despite his expertise, he seems to have entertained a peculiar view of the democratic process.

'Instead of the 1800 inhabitants of Maresfield assembling as heretofore in vestry for the transaction of their business,' he advised his audience, 'you will elect your parish council, and the 1800 will have to give way to eighteen.'

Presumably even Chambers would have conceded that these eighteen councillors would fit rather more easily into the hall than the full complement of villagers into his imaginary vestry. They would, at all events, find themselves twiddling their thumbs: 'Parish councils have very little to do. I am afraid that there will be some disappointment felt when members of the parish councils find how very narrow and restricted their powers are.'

Alas for fond hopes that the Act would encourage a crop of new libraries: the money available would buy very few books indeed. As for the idea that a rash of allotments was about to spread across the rural scene now that councils were empowered to rent or buy land for the purpose, Chambers poured scorn on such optimism.

'One man I heard of,' he related, to laughter from the hall, 'actually got the idea into his head that he was perfectly entitled to possess himself, for the purpose of an allotment, of a field that was right in front of the Squire's window!'

It was perhaps the fear of such Jacobin insolence which prompted moves to prevent a poll in several parishes. The reason given was always the expense involved, but the language used often hints at another story.

At Ninfield we come across a double act. The rector, the Rev R. A. Bennett, told villagers that 'he hoped some arrangement might be made by which a poll would be avoided, and strongly deprecated any action on the part of anyone which would lead to the parish being put to the expense of an election.' The local guardian, J. W. M. Ashby, then took the floor, supporting the rector's stand and proposing 'that they choose a committee of selection, and let that committee choose seven representatives of each class of the community.'

Divide and rule? Most of the sturdy citizens of Ninfield declared that they wanted a poll whatever their betters advised them, but at Burwash just such a selection committee was formed by a meeting of electors three weeks before the fateful day: 'The hon. secretary reported the receipt of the names of nineteen intending candidates for the thirteen places, and after considerable discussion it was decided to invite all the candidates willing or anxious to become parish councillors to meet the committee in conference in the schoolroom.

'It was hoped that in this way proportionate class representation could be arranged, and a compromise effected between conflicting interests, so that a list of names that would enjoy the confidence of the electors could be submitted to the parish meeting on December 4th.'

This manoeuvre, while no doubt legally acceptable, was surely nothing but a shameless attempt to stitch up the result by those who feared the consequences of *dis*proportionate class representation.

Had Henry Lane considered such tactics at Westmeston? Certainly he must have discussed the dire possibilities with men he trusted and drawn up a plan of action for the forthcoming meeting. The question was whether they would be overwhelmed nonetheless by rampant hordes of serfs eager to give a bloody nose to their betters. Lane, after all, was not a popular man. The locals, though none would have dared to hint as much in his hearing, thought him distinctly eccentric. And was their loyalty not tested by a lord of the manor who was seldom to be seen at New Middleton (now Middleton Manor), his handsome three-bayed manor house with its Tuscan colonnade and cladding of neat mathematical tiles? The squire preferred to spend most of the year at his London address and leave the affairs of Streat and Westmeston in the hands of his bailiff.

The Westmeston minutes, silent as to how many of the great unwashed filed into the village school that evening, are nevertheless eloquent in

The minutes of the first Westmeston parish meeting, at which the lord of the manor, Henry Lane, was appointed chairman.

their simplicity. Henry Lane must have looked on with quiet content as two of his tenant farmers (Botting of Place Farm, Springett of Hayleigh Farm) successively, and successfully, proposed and seconded 'that the Rev Sclater take the chair'. So far, so good: business as usual.

Now Botting, who was related to Lane and paid only a peppercorn rent for his land, stood up to propose 'that there be no parish council', and this was seconded — surprise, surprise! — by Lane's own trusty bailiff, George Mills. Springett (his name appearing as 'Springate' in the written record) then proposed that Lane be appointed chairman. Carried unanimously; end of meeting; QED.

But what was happening in other parts of East Sussex at this moment? Council minutes and newspaper reports give a vivid and often entertaining insight into the tensions of the time. Occasionally these were purely personal: the first meeting at Ewhurst opened with a bout of sparring between neighbours, with Mr Reader asking Mr Peirce 'if he would undertake to cease letting his meadows to roundabout people' and an obdurate Mr Peirce replying 'that he would cease to do so if our county councillor ceased to cart on the roads in wet weather'.

Other incidents, however, reveal something of the hopes and frustrations of the ordinary man, and the fears and disdain of his former rulers who were being forced to go through the motions of democratic reform. At Rye Foreign, where the successful candidates included a JP, a farmer and the vicar, the disappointed Mr Ashdown (seven votes; not elected) 'said he did not think a very representative body had been chosen. He understood all classes were to be represented.' The tart reply from the chairman, Colonel Brookfield, was that 'he would not express any opinion about parish councils'.

Not every man of the cloth was opposed to an election: not, at any rate, once he had witnessed the initial show of hands. At Iden, where the Rev. J. L. Bates failed to win a seat, he demanded a poll, 'pointing out that, as only 40 electors were present, they could not claim to represent the entire parish; besides which, the method of taking the votes was absurd, and he hoped the Government would devise a better plan before next year.'

The system which he found ridiculous gave villagers seven votes each because there were seven seats on the council. But the disgruntled man of the cloth went further in his complaint: 'It was quite evident that some of those present had voted more than seven times.'

It is at Maresfield that we have perhaps the clearest, and certainly the most amusing, clash between the old order and the new. The rector, the Rev. J. B. M. Butler, launching the parish meeting with an unbearably pompous speech to the effect that he had chaired the vestry meetings for 18 years from nothing more than a desire to serve, told a packed hall that this occasion would always be remembered in the annals of the parish.

'He would only say,' reported the *Sussex Express,* 'that he looked upon it as an honour and a privilege . . . to be allowed to stand at the helm and steer the old ship into the new course that was before them (*applause*). And he was quite confident that if any difficulties occurred, and they might well occur, they might rely upon the old crew (*renewed applause*).

After thirteen councillors had been chosen from 22 candidates on a show of hands, Butler 'hoped and trusted' that the villagers would 'save the expenditure of money, time and feeling' by electing the thirteen without a contest.'

At this point Frederick Jenner stood up. He was only a humble gardener, and he was to show the expected deference when addressing his betters, but he had come 14th in the voting and he was damned if he was going to accept the rector's suggestion. Jenner demanded a poll.

THE CHAIRMAN: Well, of course you are entitled to it. I hadn't ought to discourage you, but I am sorry.

MR JENNER: I'm not the only one, sir. It's not satisfactory to a great many. (A VOICE: 'It's not merely one, Mr Butler.')

MR WM. STEVENSON complained that not more than half the parish knew anything about the meeting, and that it was not sufficient to put up the notices on church and chapel doors. People did not go to church to look at public notices, and many had not seen those announcing this particular meeting.

THE CHAIRMAN: We can't help that. This is a parish meeting, not a religious meeting.

MR STEVENSON: It hasn't been done fair. The notices ought to be put up alongside the road, so that people could see them as they passed by. They would go to church and wouldn't see them.

THE CHAIRMAN: We can't help that, Stevenson. They have acted in accordance with the legal directions.

MR STEVENSON: Quite so; but it's unfair.

THE CHAIRMAN: Well, you must talk to the people who make the law.

CAPTAIN NOBLE: I should like to point out to Mr Stevenson that those people who did not see the notice at church or chapel could have seen one on Mr Turner's oasthouse, and it is sticking there now.

MR STEVENSON: I didn't see it.

MR LAWRENCE (to Stevenson): How came you here then? (*loud laughter*).

THE CHAIRMAN said the fact that there were so many present was very good proof that the meeting was widely known. A poll had been demanded, and if it was insisted on he must signify the same to the Returning Officer. MR JENNER alleged that the meeting had been 'packed' by certain parties in order to outvote the small tenants (*applause from the back of the room*).

THE CHAIRMAN: I don't think you have any right to say that.

MR JENNER: It's a fact, sir (*hear, hear and interruption*).

THE CHAIRMAN: On whose behalf do you demand a poll? For yourself?

MR JENNER: No, sir.

THE CHAIRMAN: Because some of these candidates will withdraw in order to save the parish the expense and bother of an election.

MR JENNER: I shall not withdraw.

CAPTAIN NOBLE and MR MARK SANDFORD then announced their willingness to withdraw the candidates they had nominated (Messrs ENOCH TYLER and JOSEPH RIDLEY respectively) with the view of settling matters amicably.

THE CHAIRMAN: That will bring in our friend Jenner. Would that satisfy him?

MR BISHOP said he did not think they ought to get rid of such good men.

CAPTAIN NOBLE: I think I may say, both for myself and Mr Sandford, that if a poll is forced we will neither withdraw. They are both eminently fit men to sit on the parish council, and we only withdrew their names to save a contest.

MR F. BARCHARD said, on the same grounds, he would withdraw in favour of Jenner.

THE CHAIRMAN: The question is whether that would save a poll, or is there anybody else who wishes to insist on a poll?

In reply to the Rector, JENNER said he would withdraw his demand for a poll. Some animated discussion followed at the back of the room, and eventually MR WM TURNER came to the front and said he should demand a poll.

THE CHAIRMAN: Very well; that settles it, and there must be a poll.

The outcome, happy to relate, was that both Frederick Jenner and William Turner (a corn and brick merchant) were eventually elected to Maresfield parish council, while the insufferable Captain Noble — one of the thirteen originally chosen by show of hands — suffered a less than noble defeat.

Polls, whatever their expense, were demanded in a great many parishes, and voting took place around the middle of the month. Despite the forecast in a *Sussex Express* leader that there would be few contested elections, there was a veritable rush of nominations. In Wadhurst, for example, there were as many as 48 candidates at the outset, although a few were later to withdraw, while 45 would-be councillors contested the fifteen seats at Rotherfield.

Unfortunately the weather was bad. For the Rotherfield elections (which also involved Burnt Oak, Jarvis Brook, Crowborough, Eridge and part of Groombridge), there was little better than a steady trickle of voters for most of the day, and this must have been at least in part due to the fog and rain 'which soon reduced the roads (good as they are) to sloppy mud'. At Burwash the response was regarded as disappointing, since only 216 of the 378 electors registered a vote, although that 54 turnout rate would seem quite heartening today.

The make-up of Rotherfield's council must have been largely to the satisfaction of the old ruling class: there were two gentlemen and six farmers, a couple of grocers, a builder and a butcher. The three other places, however, were taken by a bricklayer and two labourers. Do we sense here a hint of something stirring among the hayricks?

We do, if only in a small way, and it is surely not fanciful to look back to the so-called Swing Riots of 1831, when an earlier agricultural depression brought a spate of machine-breaking and incendiarism to the south-east. The rioting spread throughout Sussex then, but it began in Brede and was concentrated largely in the east of the county where there were few of the great all-controlling family estates which could be found in the west: Petworth, Goodwood, Arundel and their like.

In 1894 the upsetting of the rural applecart seems to have been most pronounced in those earlier areas of discontent. Of the seven councillors elected to Brede parish council, for instance, only one was a farmer. The exact status of contemporary trades and occupations is difficult to gauge, but there seems to have been a pretty democratic spread in the rest of the council: a labourer, a butcher, a carrier, a carpenter, a roadman, a shoemaker and an insurance agent.

We find labourers voted on to several councils in this area, although always in small minorities. At Icklesham there was a single labourer alongside a surgeon, the foreman of the stone works, a carrier, a grocer, a shipwright, a

SATURDAY, NOVEMBER 3, 1894.

THE NEW LOCAL GOVERNMENT ACT.

· THE FORTHCOMING ELECTIONS.

The Parish Councils Act—as it is popularly called—the mode in which the elections under it are to be carried out and by whom, and the effects that may possibly be produced by the Act when it is in full working order, continue to furnish topics for conversation and discussion, especially in rural districts. In urban communities, on the other hand, we fail to learn that the question is exciting more than passing and languid interest. It has been pointed out that the anomalies with which our whole system of local as well as national government bristles, so far from having been reduced by recent legislation have really been increased. We have already alluded to the inconsistency, for instance, of allowing married women to vote at parochial and district elections, but not at municipal elections, although women living in towns are quite as intelligent and as capable of exercising the franchise as their married sisters and cousins residing in the country. But another anomaly quite as glaring has arisen from the fact that numerical population has been taken as the basis which must guide county councils in fixing the number of councillors acting in parishes and

A leader in the Conservative-leaning Sussex Express *a month before the first parish elections, predicting that 'it will be difficult in some places to find sufficient residents qualified to act.' In the event there were large numbers of candidates in many parishes.*

market gardener, three farmers and an independent. The two labourers at Westfield sat round a table with three farmers, two gentlemen, an innkeeper and an engineer. At Mayfield there was one labourer on a council of sixteen, his companions being three farmers, two farmer/millers, two innkeepers and one each of grocer, ironmonger, carpenter, tailor, farm bailiff, wheelwright/ builder, joiner/carpenter and gardener. Further west, at Alfriston, a solitary labourer pitched his influence against that of a gentleman, a builder, a saddler, a grocer, a blacksmith and a horse trainer. Few diehard vestry supporters can have resisted the temptation to praise a new order which offered such tokens of democracy while changing little.

At Burwash, where the selection committee had been notified of nineteen nominations, there were in fact 27 candidates by the time the poll was held. At the parish meeting the lower orders had evidently had a modest success, but the wider electorate took a different view — although, for the *Sussex Express,* the newsworthiness of the occasion failed to promote it above the fortnightly meeting of the rat and sparrow club at the Rose & Crown Hotel, where bounty hunters had fetched no fewer than 507 rats' tails and 365 sparrows' heads.

In any event, 'the noteworthy features were the rejection of the labourers' candidates and the reversing of the show of hands taken at the previous meeting.'

With hindsight we can see that the fears of Gladstone's critics were wildly exaggerated. That unashamed (and startlingly recent) description of ordinary country people as 'peasants' provides a major explanatory clue: no legislation can of itself change deeply-entrenched attitudes, and the rural poor were accustomed to subservience. The barrister J. Morrison Davidson, publishing a pamphlet to alert 'the new rulers of rural England' to their exciting opportunities, had nevertheless included a prescient warning: 'It is not easy to extract the corroding iron of centuries of custom from the minds of the best of us.'

So it was to be in many a small, closed community like Henry Lane's. With initial voting by show of hands it took a brave soul to demand a poll. How, realistically, could humble working men, many of them illiterate and without the slightest experience of decision-making beyond their own personal sphere, be expected to thwart the wishes of the people who put food in their stomachs and clothes on their backs? (And which woman in those times, we might add, would stand for election if her menfolk were against such a bluestocking notion? Here we should salute two pioneers who went down to honourable, inevitable defeat: Miss Warmington at Rotherfield and Mrs Mary Britton at Mayfield).

Many of the labouring poor were, in any case, content to accept the benefits of a near-feudal system if the squire was, by the standards of the day, benevolent. Henry Lane, to do him justice, had been among these more enlightened landlords, turning the horses out of his stables in order to create cottages for the grooms and carters and their families. This chronic culture of deference is strikingly expressed in a tombstone at Herstmonceux to Richard Morris, 'who himself desired it might be remembered that he owed his Bread to his Grace the Duke of Newcastle

'Mr C. Mannington proposed and Mr J. H. Houseman seconded,' read the minutes of the first meeting of Ewhurst parish council on December 29, 1894, 'that the clerk do obtain a bag for the parish books at a cost not exceeding 30s. Carried unanimously, all voting.' That leather bag, with the words PARISH COUNCIL OF EWHURST SUSSEX on the back, was still being used by the chairman, Alan Bowden, in the centenary year.

his great benefactor': that inscription is from a rather earlier age, but the sentiments would have been recognisable to many in 1894.

We only have to consider the parishes of Ashburnham and Penhurst (today combined, but then separate entities) to recognise the impossibility of genuine reform. An extreme case, no doubt, but these villages were totally controlled by the Earl of Ashburnham — and were to remain effectively under that family's paternalistic thumb, for good or ill, until large parts of the estate were sold to pay for death duties as recently as the 1950s.

It should surprise nobody to learn that Mr Anchitel P. Ashburnham was the first chairman of Ashburnham parish council and that the Earl was one of the seven councillors; or that the Rev. Charles Baker should be the chairman of the Penhurst parish meeting, he and his successor holding that post into the first world war. When every house, the school, the village hall, the almshouses, the pub and the shop were provided by the ruling family; when every job derived from the estate; when the system of control was such that 'difficult' families were moved to a kind of penal settlement in the woods near Penhurst; how, in these circumstances, could there be any meaningful stirrings of independence? A more common response to rural depression and suppression was to move to the towns or to emigrate.

Leaf through the records of those parishes for which the last vestry minutes have survived and one fact leaps from the pages: the people running local affairs after 1894 were substantially the same as those who were in charge before. They were all men, and most of them men of substance. Lord Monk-Bretton, for example, was chairman of Barcombe parish council, Thomas Baden Powell his counterpart at Newick. The election of the village grocer, Harry Norman, as chairman of Falmer parish council in 1894 may suggest (no doubt erroneously) a levelling spirit at work in that tied community, but within two years the Earl of Chichester, who ruled the area from Stanmer House, had replaced him. At Whatlington, in March 1900, we find the parish meeting actually being held in the home of the former churchwarden and overseer William Ashby, still evidently an unchallenged leader of his community.

Newcomers there obviously were, but not of the kind who might rock the boat. The breakdown of councillors at Chailey in 1897 is fairly typical: two gentlemen, four farmers, one veterinary surgeon/farmer, one baker and one brick and tile maker. Ninfield returned a JP, a farmer, two market gardeners, a miller and a bricklayer, while the council at Northiam comprised two farmers, a surgeon, a solicitor, a builder, a licenced victualler, a grocer, a baker and a mail contractor. Four of Ewhurst's nine members were farmers, the others being two gentlemen, a schoolmaster, an innkeeper and a butcher.

The church retained its position in such villages, too. At Arlington the Rev. Thomas Bunston stepped down from the chair but acted as vice-chairman until 1919, a length of service which was by no means unusual. The vicar of Peasmarsh, the Rev. W. R. Brodrick ('held in high esteem by all classes,' read a newspaper report), assumed the council chairmanship the day after his 79th birthday. The Rev. Clement Powell was returned as a councillor at Newick, having stood as an independent, although he had apparently received most of his support from the Conservatives.

And yet, this profound rural conservatism acknowledged, it is surely in order to give at least one-and-a-half cheers for democracy. Consider for instance, those entries in the Penhurst minute book, the first of them in December 1899, which show illiterate labourers making their 'mark' alongside the signatures of the community's leaders. At this distance of time it is impossible to know whether such men were simply drafted in to make up the numbers or whether they were genuinely interesting themselves in parish affairs. What we can say, however, is that they were undoubtedly learning the basic lessons of local government and public accountability: they were becoming citizens.

The majority of Gladstone's peasants may have failed to man the barricades, but a vital principle had been established. And if the revolution remained merely potential, awaiting the social changes that would be brought about by two world wars, there had, at least, been a colourful dress rehearsal. One day, as yet far off, the curtain would rise in earnest.

Henry Lane, meanwhile, settled into an untroubled chairmanship of Westmeston parish meeting which would last for eleven years — during which considerable stretch of time he attended but a single meeting.

The minutes of a parish meeting at Penhurst in 1899 were signed by the chairman and two overseers, with Richard Crump inscribing 'his mark'. Was the illiterate Crump merely brought in to make up the numbers or was he, in the true spirit of Gladstone's reforms, a humble labourer determined to have his say in parish affairs?

THE PARISHES AT WAR

After twenty years of uneasy slumber Gladstone's civic warriors woke to the sound of distant gunfire. Those two decades had seen a continuing decline in the countryside and, since they derived their revenues principally from rates on agricultural land, the councils had found themselves both poor and ineffective. Now, swiftly drained of their youngest and fittest men, the villages of East Sussex would all too soon suffer shortages of food and coal, not to mention a dreadful toll of human sacrifice. Their world was about to change utterly.

To dip into the parish council archives for 1914-18 is to find the Great War plotted in erratic, but vivid, minor detail. We may indeed be reminded of G. F. Chambers's assertion that 'parish councils have very little to do' (an impression reinforced by a meeting at Ringmer in January, 1915, when the clerk, a single councillor and two press reporters organised an impromptu card party while waiting in vain for a quorum), but the fact that the fledgling 'rural parliaments' were for the most part helpless bystanders gives an extra force to the occasional striking item from minute books still busy, when at all, with footpath and hedgerow matters.

So faint are the rumblings of war in the pre-1916 records that the conflict might almost be imaginary: how terrible then, and how terribly moving, to have this silence abruptly broken by an expression of condolence to a councillor who has lost his son. Later entries are similarly episodic, and telling: appeals to the local food controller for a fairer distribution of meat; calculations of the required numbers of 'homes for heroes'; plans for suitable war memorials.

Some entries suggest rather more than they make plain. The Burwash response to a request for army volunteers seems to bristle with barely-concealed fury, while Alfriston's objection to being put out of bounds to the troops (a fate the council had itself innocently invited) surely had a financial motive which it would have been shameful to acknowledge.

Herstmonceux. July 19, 1915
The chairman read a circular from the emergency committee suggesting that farmers should not crowd their stacks round farm buildings, and that the parish councils might be asked to organise this and salvage parties to act in case of air raids. Having a fire brigade in the district, it was not thought necessary to do anything in the matter.

Hadlow Down. April 20, 1916
The chairman moved and Mr Ashdown seconded that a vote of sympathy with the vice chairman on the loss of his son who was fighting for his country be recorded.

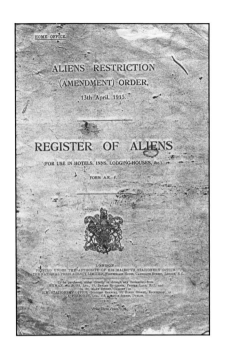

Crowlink Farmhouse, near Friston, was used to house 'aliens' during the first world war. This page from the register records Danish, French and Swiss nationals who were passing through, their occupations ranging from tractor driver and lady's help to French teacher, journalist and musician. Their strange names were clearly something of a trial to the poor soul given the task of writing them down.

Westfield, May 2, 1916
Letter to Rev. E. J. Morgan: 'On behalf of the chairman and members of the Westfield parish council, I have to express to you and your family their great regret at hearing of your great loss, and also to offer you all their most sincere sympathies in your great sorrow and sad bereavement.'

Heathfield. July 18, 1916
'That on the approach of the second anniversary of a declaration of a righteous war, this meeting of the parish council of Heathfield records once more its inflexible determination to continue to a victorious end the struggle to maintain that ideal of liberty and justice which is the common and sacred cause of the Allies.'

Hailsham. July 21, 1916
The clerk reported that Mrs Breed has asked for the permission of the council to erect a seat for wounded soldiers in the High Street opposite St Wilfrid's. Ordered that the letter be sent on to the county surveyor with a letter stating that the subject has the sympathy of this council.

Forest Row. August 15, 1916
A letter was read from the military authorities, asking if the council had any objection to the river south of the railway station being dammed and used as a bathing station for the troops. The chairman reported that he had instructed the clerk to reply that the council had no objection provided that the spot is adequately screened as a protection for the public.

Hadlow Down. January 2, 1917
A vote of sympathy with Mr Garton on the loss of his son in fighting for his country was proposed by the chairman and unanimously carried.

Burwash. January 11, 1917
Letter to East Sussex War Agricultural Committee: 'With reference to your communication of 1st January, 1917, I beg to inform you that a special meeting of the Burwash Parish Council the supreme importance of increasing the supply of potatoes was discussed. It was decided that a circular should be printed and distributed amongst all the cottagers holding an allotment or small garden, and individual councillors agreed to take upon themselves a house to house visitation, and to impress upon our population the grave necessity of increasing our food supply in the coming summer.'

The 6th City of London Rifles, known as 'The Cast-iron Sixth' because they were the only regiment in the British Army to sport a black badge, marching through Newick in 1915 on their way to the new camp at Crowborough. Newick itself lost 28 men in the war.

Udimore. January 11, 1917
'As there are no allotments or small holdings in this parish, this council is of the opinion that any increase in the growth of potatoes during the coming year must necessarily rest with the farmers, as they are the only ones who hold land to put under cultivation for the object. Practically all the cottagers save their own seed.'

Arlington. January 18, 1917
'This council regrets to report that there appears to be no prospect of increasing the growth of potatoes owing to the price fixed for the produce.'

Pett. January 18, 1917
Mr Dunlop read a letter he had received from Mr Walter F. Ingram, chairman of the East Sussex War Agricultural Committee relating to the potato disease and the best way of preventing it, and at the same time increasing the crop by the use of sprayers as recommended by Mr Goring, horticulturalist to the East Sussex County Council. The kind of sprayer recommended as being most suitable for small growers was the Bucket Sprayer, which would cost about £1. After some discussion it was decided to purchase a Bucket Sprayer.

Burwash. March, 1917
Letter to Mr G. N. Osborne: 'Your circular letter relative to the Volunteer Forces was laid before the Burwash parish council at a special meeting held 28/2/17, when it received attentive consideration. The council begs to bring to your notice that the parish of Burwash, which includes Burwash Weald, is entirely agricultural. There is no manufacture or handicraft carried on within its boundaries.

The population at the last census was 2,148, made up of 1,074 males and 1,074 females. The parish has sent 372 men to the colours, of whom 39 have already given their lives for their country. This works out to the very high percentage of 34.6 of the total male population from babies to old men.

Practically every able-bodied man from 18 to 41 has joined the army, with the exception of those exempted for agricultural necessity, and a very few who have received extended exemption from the tribunals.

It is not too much to say that almost every man over age for active military duty is engaged in some communal work which absorbs all his time. So deficient is labour that the council is looking forward with anxiety to the elucidation of how the cottage gardens and allotments of the men now with the colours are to be cultivated.

The expectation that men, many of them in advanced middle age, after a full day's labour would give up the cultivation of their gardens and allotments and walk six or eight miles to attend drills is unlikely to be realised.

The parish council, conscious of the patriotism of its parishioners, for ninety per cent of its army roll are voluntary enlistments, feels that it would be uncandid if it held out expectation of any appreciable number joining a local volunteer unit.'

Udimore. March 23, 1917
'That this being a purely agricultural village, this council does not consider it necessary to canvass the parish for National Service enrolment, as they are of the opinion that men who are employed in agricultural work are engaged in an essentially important branch of National Service; and that owing to the present great shortage of labour, it would be a serious calamity for employees to be drafted elsewhere.'

Alfriston. March 26, 1917
A letter was received from A. S. Haynes Esq of White Court stating that he had in store about 35 bushels of potatoes which he has kept for the purpose of supplying the needs of some of the poorer families in Alfriston during the time when potatoes will be practically unobtainable by them, and other staple foodstuffs much increased in price. The distribution to be arranged by the parish council, the sale price to be one penny a pound.

Heathfield. March 27, 1917
The chairman stated that an offer of about ten bushels of seed potatoes at the sale of £9 per ton had been received from Heathfield Park.

Ticehurst. March 27, 1917
A letter had been received from a ratepayer calling attention to the extreme shortness of labour on the farms in this district, suggesting that the councils be asked to dispense with most of the roadmen during the summer months.

Alfriston. April 18, 1917
Letter to the Officer Commanding Canadian Forces, the Camp, Seaford. 'I am directed by this council to inform you that about nine on Thursday evening a Canadian soldier was seen to climb the village cross stone here with the result that the stone collapsed and the man fell on the

road, sustaining apparently considerable injuries to his head.

I am to say that the village extremely regrets the damage to their ancient cross-stone, and while they are pleased their village should be available for a little change for the men in their leisure time, I am to respectfully express the hope that efficient steps will be taken, by patrol or otherwise, to ensure as much as possible the keeping of order for the future.'

Pett. April 19, 1917

Mr Dunlop, in referring to the recent air raid at Cliff End, called attention to the situation of the search light apparatus in close proximity to so many houses and buildings, and suggested that a letter should be sent to the War Office, asking that the search light might be moved to some spot more distant from human habitation.

The market cross at Alfriston, demolished by a lorry in more recent times, was damaged by a roistering Canadian soldier in April 1917, with the result that the village was declared out of bounds to the troops.

Arlington. July 12, 1917

'Resolved that Arlington being a scattered parish, a rat and sparrow club would be difficult to work. The farmers be requested to do all they can to destroy rats and house sparrows on their farms.'

Hartfield. October 5, 1917

Some discussion arose as to the unequal distribution of meat, and the clerk was asked to write to the local food control committee, asking that steps should be taken if possible to secure a more equitable division.

Westfield. January 23, 1918

'As there is a shortage of meat, butter, margarine, tea, bacon and matches in the local shops, the Westfield parish council ask if the Battle food controller can do anything to obtain a fair supply, and would also recommend that the local shops be asked to supply customers on the Government rations basis.'

Hooe. January 24, 1918
Margarine, butter, lard. 'That the council draw the food controller's attention to the absence of the above necessary commodities in this parish, our local retailer of these articles having only obtained 16lbs of margarine and a small quantity of lard since November last. The lack of those foods is causing considerable privation, especially to children.'

Heathfield. March 12, 1918
'That the whole or part of the recreation ground at Punnetts Town be let out to parishioners in allotments at a nominal rent for a term not exceeding five years.'

Westfield. March 15, 1918
Letter to the food controller. 'The supply in the parish is in a very unsatisfactory state, especially in the matter of meat, as last week there was not any meat at all in the local butcher's shop till Saturday, owing — in the opinion of the parish council — to the bad management of the shop, and the utter neglect of the business in general by the proprietor.

The council further wish me to ask if the local food control committee could not intercede on their behalf so that the parishioners should obtain a fairer supply and not be punished — as at present — by the proprietor of this particular shop.'

Ticehurst. March 26, 1918
The chairman reported that he had caused bills to be printed, inviting applicants for allotments. Thirteen applications were received, and fourteen plots of 10 rods each had been stumped out at Mr W. M. Balcombe's land, north of the Bell field. A draught agreement for the hire of the land by this council was produced.

Alfriston. April 19, 1918
A circular was received from the Rural League as to pig clubs and the keeping of pigs. To reply, That every effort appears being made by the inhabitants to increase the number of pigs and poultry.

Westfield. May 12, 1919
Celebrations of peace. The chairman (Major A. C. Sayers) suggested that the lead should be taken by the parish council, remarking that his own personal feelings were against any festivities. Cllr Fowler proposed something to be done for the children, to give them a good day.

Cllr Miss Cooper thought an enjoyable afternoon with sports, to be followed by tea for the children, would be a good thing.

Alfriston. May 17, 1918
Letter to the Commanding Officer, Canadian Forces: 'The above council much regret that Alfriston is still out of bounds to the forces under your command and, acting under the expressed wish of nearly the whole of the inhabitants, we respectfully ask you to use your best endeavours to have the restriction withdrawn.'

Hailsham. September 6, 1918
Housing of the Working Classes Act. The council discussed the matter of house accommodation in the parish and unanimously arrived at the conclusion that at least 50 small houses were required in the Hailsham ward of the parish.

The parish councils played an organising role in the erection of war memorials throughout the county. Wadhurst's records the death of 114 villagers during the first world war, the inscription reading: 'Let those that come after see that they be not forgotten'.

Arlington. September 19, 1918
'Resolved, that there appeared to be sufficient cottages in the parish before the war, but there may be a demand for six or eight more for agricultural purposes after the war. These should be provided by the owners of the various farms that appear to need them.'

Ticehurst. October 8, 1918
The only likely need for extra houses is in the district of Stonegate, where six are required for railway employees. The council suggest that these might be provided by the railway company.

Hailsham. November 28, 1918
War memorial. 'That the council take the initiative for providing by public subscription a permanent memorial for the men of Hailsham who made

Falmer's war memorial had a practical use — until the rapid spread of the motor car, at least. The horse trough was restored in 1985, local craftsman Owen Williams (left) sculpting a new inscription: IN MEMORY OF THE 1914-18 WAR. His wife Doris (second left), still a parish councillor in the centenary year, was Falmer's first woman chairman. (An Evening Argus photograph)

the supreme sacrifice in the great world war while serving in His Majesty's forces upholding the cause of freedom and justice.'

Hadlow Down. December 4, 1918

A letter was read from Uckfield RDC, stating that they had a small amount of coal for disposal, and asking this council to find out what amount was urgently needed to supply the wants of the poorer inhabitants of the parish.

Ticehurst. January 14, 1919

War memorial. It having been suggested to some members of this council that Ticehurst should join with Wadhurst in a hospital scheme, this idea was unanimously negatived.

Alfriston. January 20, 1919

'That the attention of the fuel controller be drawn to the serious shortage of the supply to the village, in many cases families having been for days without any coal.'

22

Herstmonceux. March 24, 1919
'That the chairman call a public meeting to discuss the arrangements for the celebration of peace.'

Rotherfield. March 31, 1919
War memorial committee. It was finally resolved at this stage to call a public meeting to report the various proposals, and to recommend the following as a suitable and practicable war memorial: 1 A brass or bronze plaque, suitably inscribed, to be fixed in the parish church; 2 To reconstruct and improve the Institute; 3 If sufficient funds available, to provide a memorial cross on a suitable site in the village.

Hartfield. April 15, 1919
The council came to the conclusion that twelve houses would meet the present demand, viz four at Holtye, two in Coleman's Hatch and six in Hartfield.

Udimore. July 9, 1919
Peace celebrations. The chairman outlined the following programme for the day: 1 Service at the parish church in the morning; 2 Children's sports in the afternoon; 3 Children's tea; 4 Tea for the adults of the village; 5 Sports for adults; 6 Fireworks (to be provided by Major B. V. Mair and himself).

Burwash. October 15, 1919
War trophies. A letter from W. Fricker, Secretary of the Sussex Volunteer Force Association, that he had been instructed by Lord Leconfield to forward six rifles and asking for the address to whom the articles should be sent. The rifles had been received by Cllr Feilden, and he produced one and suggested that they be kept at the Institute. The clerk was directed to write to the Secretary of the Institute Council, asking if they could be deposited.

Arlington. October 30, 1919
Resolved that in the opinion of the council, houses are much needed at Arlington Street and Caneheath.

Udimore. November 3, 1919
A letter from the East Sussex County Council on the subject of holding two supplementary rat weeks with a view to concerted action was brought to the notice of members. After fully discussing the matter it was resolved to let the matter lie on the table, as the few rats to be found in the parish do not call for any active measures.

Burwash. November 3, 1920

War trophies. A letter from Cllr Feilden drawing attention to this matter, and stating that he wished to be released of the custody of them was read, and after discussing the matter it was resolved that the clerk ask the Secretary of the Institute for a prompt reply as to these trophies.

Burwash. March 30, 1921

War trophies. A letter from the Secretary of the Institute was read, as follows:

'Dear Sir, Your letter in reference to the German rifles belonging to the parish council has been laid before the council of the Burwash Institute who request me to say that they regret they cannot see their way to accept them. Yours faithfully . . .'

After some discussion it was proposed by Cllr Jarvis and seconded by Cllr Finlayson that they be offered to the managers of the school, and if all or any of them be not accepted that they be broken up. Carried unanimously.

Burwash. July 18, 1921

German rifles. The following letter was read:

'Dear Sir, I informed the School Managers of the kind offer of German rifles from the Burwash parish council, for which they are much obliged, and which they regret that they are unable to accept. I am, yours faithfully . . .'

Cllr Malpass was then asked to take the rifles and break them up according to arrangements made at a previous meeting.

ALL HANDS TO THE PUMP!

Local pride may encourage people to emphasise their differences from those in the next village, but cooperation between parishes is quite common, too — and not only in times of war. Herbert Newbery *was brought up with stories of Battle's fire brigade, because his father (also Herbert) served as its captain for many years from the 1920s. As he relates here, the parishes around Battle put their hands in their pockets to help provide the very first motorised fire engine.*

It must have been a hundred years ago or more that Battle acquired its first fire engine of any kind — a red monster built by Merrieweathers of London. The hose was made of leather, oil-dressed, and it was held together by a great many copper rivets so that a 50ft length weighed a considerable amount and took up quite a lot of room. When it was fully loaded with firemen the engine weighed well over two tons and two heavy horses were needed to pull it.

Fires, I think, were rather treated as a game in those times. I have no record or knowledge of the crew, but I do know that the officer in charge was the clerk to the local council.

The original fire station still exists at the rear of 40 High Street — now the yard of Jempsons the undertakers but formerly known as Fire Station Yard. Even today you can see the ladder racks and the well for filling the engine.

It took some time to gather all this lot together when the fire alarm was given, and what happened to Normanhurst in 1908 is a good illustration of that. This was the mansion built by Earl Brassey, the railway engineer, on the Battle-Catsfield border.

Normanhurst caught light, and the Battle and Bexhill brigades were called. It took Battle just over half an hour to get there, and Bexhill arrived about three-quarters of an hour later. Needless to say, a large part of the mansion was destroyed. After Earl Brassey rebuilt it, he bought a steamer — that is, a steam-driven pump — which was manned by his own staff.

We'll now take a jump to the early 1920s, when the clerk to the council retired and was replaced by F. C. Sheppard. The fact was that Sheppard knew nothing about fire brigades, and he didn't want the job. One of my uncles was on the council at the time and he put my father's name forward as a likely Captain, he being a local builder of many years experience.

After much pushing, my father undertook the job of running the brigade. He went through the personnel and got rid of those he thought were useless, replacing them with men he knew. They were mostly builders, and they were given some drilling. All firemen were volunteers in those days, unless they were in large cities, and this is what they were paid per annum:

Memories of Normanhurst. The over-large window in the house known as Pulpitt Gate at the foot of All Saints Street, Hastings, came from Lord Brassey's mansion at Catsfield. The house, restored after the fire of 1908, was dismantled in 1954.

Captain	£2	0s 0d
Lieutenant	£1	15s 0d
Foreman & Engineer	£1	0s 0d
Firemen		15s 0d
Call Boy		10s 0d

When they attended fires their pay was as follows:

Officers	5s for the first hour
	3s for each succeeding hour
Foreman & Engineer	2s 6d per hour
Firemen	2s 3d per hour
Call Boy	1s per hour
Helpers	1s 4d per hour

You'll perhaps wonder what the 'helpers' were for. Well, the fire engine, being manually operated, took eight men each side to man the pump. They pumped for ten minutes and rested for twenty, so you can see that it was a tough job. There was never any shortage of volunteers, but as many as 48 were needed for the pumping: sixteen in three shifts.

They couldn't, of course, have horses on permanent standby, so they had to borrow them from local stables. The nearest one was at the foot of Battle Hill, with the engine house being close to the roundabout.

As you'll imagine, it took some time to assemble the crew and the necessary horse-power. Owing to this difficulty with the horses, my father arranged for towing eyes to be fixed on the backs of two coal lorries, and a special fitment, a tow bar, was made in Battle Forge in Mount Street. This was to be permanently attached to the fire engine.

One or two fires were safely dealt with in this way, but one call-out to Kitchenham Farm, Ashburnham, was less successful, because when they got there they found that the wooden hubs of the wheels were smouldering because of friction from the axles.

The crew used to be roused by two Call Boys, who had to go round by bicycle or on foot and knock the men up. This obviously wasn't very quick, so some thought was given to finding a speedier method of sounding the alarm. Hastings used a maroon, and I think this was Bexhill's method, too. However, my father, being something of an amateur electrician, had the idea of persuading the Post Office Telephones to connect a bell at each fireman's dwelling to be powered from a central point.

Battle's first motorised fire engine, a Dennis, in front of Battle Abbey. All of the surrounding parish councils made contributions towards its purchase. Herbert Newbery senior stands to the right of the picture, proudly to attention.

Then the question arose: what central point? Well, he managed to persuade the Chief Constable to have a generator on the desk in the police station, and this scheme worked wonderfully well. They had a weekly drill each Monday evening, and at six o'clock the duty policeman operated the bells so that, when the men arrived at seven, they could report whether all the bells were working. This system functioned so well that I believe it was adopted in other parts of the country.

Motor engines had begun to appear by this time, and my father asked the council if Battle could have one. He was told that there was no chance whatsoever unless he could raise the money, so this was a job he promptly undertook.

He had the idea of going to all the parish councils at their periodic meetings and putting the suggestion to them. This was the deal: if they would contribute towards an engine, he would cover the parish against fire. Remember that there was no fire cover at all in the country areas: if a blaze couldn't be put out with buckets of water it had to burn itself out.

So he went round to all the parishes — Crowhurst, Catsfield, Ninfield, Ashburnham and so on, a circle right round Battle — and they all contributed. Every one, without a single exception. It meant that in something like two years Battle was able to obtain its first engine.

It was a small Dennis, a marvellous little machine that did sterling work. Prior to this, my father had asked for a canvas hose to replace the old leather one, which was too short and had had too many bursts to be properly repairable. This was where I came in. Lengths of canvas hose were obtained and, to save money, he undertook to remove the old couplings from the leather hose and put them on the new one. He and I spent many hours together doing this.

My father was also mindful of the large houses in the area, so he approached Hastings and Bexhill volunteer brigades and suggested that they help each other in times of emergency. The two councils had to approve this first, of course. The brigades held drills and exercises together, and it turned out to be a very useful arrangement because on January 31, 1931, Battle Abbey caught fire, and much of it would have been destroyed if it hadn't been for this cooperation.

Battle and the brigades generally were local heroes over this. Had a fire of this magnitude taken place today I think it would have been an area call-out, with many more appliances than the three which actually attended. My father's report on the fire shows that the Battle brigade stood by until as late as the afternoon of February 3.

In 1936, at the formation of the Battle Rural District Council, the fire brigade was greatly enlarged, and it fell to my father to oversee the erection of satellite stations manned by volunteers in the villages around. There were stations

Inspecting the damage. Local people gather before the still-smouldering walls of Battle Abbey after the fire which broke out in the early hours of January 31, 1931.

The remains of the Abbot's Hall, its roof timbers collapsed in a charred heap.

at Icklesham, Camber, Broad Oak and so on. He had to train the men, and these stations operated until the war years, when they were all brought into the National Fire Service.

My father carried on for more than two years after the outbreak of war, when he had a heart attack and died. But he was always remembered as the Father of Battle Fire Brigade. **'**

```
Fire At    B A T T L E    A B B E Y.         31st.Jan.1931.

                  Call received by me  4-50 a.m.
                  Fire Bells rang      4-53 a.m.

          When I went through the Gateway I could see that the job
was far beyond the powers of the Battle Brigade to deal with, so
I 'phoned Hastings and Bexhill.

          I could see that the heart of the fire was by an opening
leading to the Minstrel Gallery of the Abbot's Hall, and got 2
jets working to cover that opening within twelve minutes from
time of call. The roof of the Hall fired from the building
paralel with it, in under the centre lead gutter, which was right
out of reach.

          Hastings arrived at 5-27, and Bexhill 2 or 3 minutes later.

          I placed Hastings pump to work at a pond in the Abbey grounds
with instructions to bring their hose up on my right and to cover
two doors leading out of Hall into Library Wing. I placed Bexhill
on a hydrant to bring theirs up on my left, to try and stop
the fire from travelling back to the north.

          As soon as these brigades were working, I moved my men to
try and stop the fire from working into the Library Wing. I was
successful in this, but it was only a matter of minutes whether I
was able to or not, as until the roof of the Abbot's Hall fell in
Hastings were not able to get their water on to two oak doors that
were well alight. If these doors had burned through it meant
loosing this wing as well as no man could live in front of the
furnace of fire then raging.

          Meanwhile Bexhill were able to cut the fire asunder and
stop it travelling northwards, thus saving that wing.

          The fire was under control by 2 p.m. Hastings brigade I
released at 4 p.m., keeping Bexhill to help through the night; I
released them 9-30 a.m. Sunday morning and Battle brigade stood by
until 12-50 p.m. Tuesday Feb.3rd..

          The three pumps between them threw over 2,000 tons of water
and used between 7 & 8,000 feet of hose.

          I have 14 lengths of badly cut hose, 8 lengths being past
mending, and the remainder will always be giving trouble through
bursts in places that have been weakened.
```

Chief officer Herbert Newbery's report of the Battle Abbey fire.

DAD'S ARMY DAYS

For the parish councils of East Sussex the second world war was to be the 'finest hour' of their first half century. Their powers might have increased very little over the previous twenty years, but this war was far closer to home than the last, putting a premium on their unique ability to coordinate the activities of local individuals and organisations.

Council minutes reveal not only the wide range of their interests (blackout rehearsals, salvage, national savings, vegetable production and a great deal more), but a spirit of independence which occasionally leads to the digging in of heels or the voicing of protest. Guestling, for instance, finds itself unable to provide volunteers for the placing of obstructions in large fields, the terseness of the reply suggesting that no great effort has been made to comply. Pett is incensed by the army's driving standards — one particular incident seeming to justify the parish's repeated complaints.

The arrival of evacuees (sometimes referred to as 'refugees' in the early stages, until a version of political correctness wins the day) presents such obvious problems of assimilation that committees are formed to deal with 'petty disputes'. We nevertheless come across a lament from Burwash, where the influx apparently exceeds the promised quota and is straining the inhabitants to breaking point.

Women had begun to increase their representation on the parish councils during the 1920s, if only in a small way, and the trend was about to accelerate now that so many of them had proved themselves in what had hitherto been a man's world. Vera Parker presents a typical example: appointed chief air raid warden at

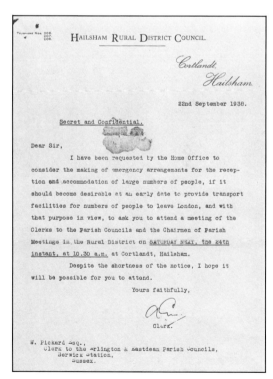

A letter to Arlington and East Dean parish councils regarding the evacuation of London. The 'secret and confidential' restriction was to be lifted within a few days.

Burwash at the beginning of the war, she is a member of the parish council by the end of it.

EAST SUSSEX COUNTY COUNCIL
AIR RAID PRECAUTIONS COMMITTEE

Demonstration
GAS-PROOFED ROOMS

Every Householder should take an early opportunity of inspecting the gas-proofed rooms at No. 28, Cliffe High Street (opposite the Odeon Theatre), Lewes.

The various types of respirators, and protective clothing for civilians officially employed on A.R.P. Duties are also on view.

ADMISSION FREE

OPEN EVERY DAY,
11.0 a.m. to 1.0 p.m., 2.0 p.m. to 4.30 p.m.
ALSO ON TUESDAY, THURSDAY & SATURDAY EVENINGS, 7.0 p.m. to 9.0 p.m.

Burwash. July 18, 1938
Miss Parker wrote thanking the council for appointing her chief warden for ARP for Burwash district. Cllr Whittaker said Miss Parker had held a meeting to show people how to fit gas masks etc.

Danehill. September 20, 1938
The chairman reported in connection with air raid precautions that the Uckfield RDC now had all the respirators required for distribution in their area, and that the memorial hall, Dane Hill, should be the centre for the fitting of gas masks and instruction in their use.

Ticehurst. October 12, 1938
It was decided that the clerk should ask the Weald Electricity Co. if they had any method established by which they could immediately extinguish the street lamp in the event of air raids.

Ditchling. October 17, 1938
Report of the air raid precautions committee: 'Gas van no. 14 visited Ditchling and 37 people passed through the van and tested the value of the respirators when exposed to tear gas. Mr Tomsett has consented to the use of a room at 15 High Street as a demonstration for a gas proof room. Suggestions for a shelter for children were made, and two spots selected, but as these were not practical it was decided that the children should be cared for in the vicinity of cellars.'

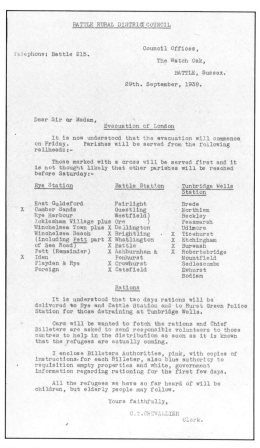

Plans for accommodating 'refugees' in the east of the county in 1938. The word often appears in parish council records at this time, but is soon to be replaced by the less demeaning 'evacuees'.

Guestling. October 13, 1938
The attention of the council was called to the necessity of forming a committee with the addition of three refugees in order to settle petty disputes between refugees and others.

Burwash. October 17, 1938
'That Miss Parker be informed that digging bombproof shelters and dug-outs was bound to cost a considerable amount of money, even when free labour were given.'

Burwash. March 20, 1939
Evacuation from London. The chairman said that Mr A. L. Bateman took the duty of chief billeting officer and with 15 visitors they had canvassed the parish and found that 385 children and 75 adults accompanying them could be accommodated. This excluded 100 children under private evacuation scheme.

Guestling. March 22, 1939
The results of the billeting in his parish for the Government Evacuation Scheme was given by the billeting officer and directed to be entered on the minutes:

Accompanied children	21
Unaccompanied children	151
Teachers/helpers/mothers	12
Adults	21
Accommodation reserved privately	143
Total	348

Burwash. July 17, 1939
Proposed from the chair, that this parish council are unanimously agreed that it was up to the Government to find blankets or to arrange that refugees should bring them, as the parish council were unable to provide them.

Guestling. July 18, 1939
The warden reported that the blackout rehearsal had been well attended and that 'everything was extremely good'.

Arlington. September 6, 1939
It was agreed to purchase a load of sand for use in case of fire caused by aerial activity during the war. To be kept at Upper Dicker.

HOUSEHOLDER'S NAME	NOTES (AS TO INCAPACITY TO TAKE ADDITIONAL PERSONS, EXEMPTIONS, REFUSALS, ETC.)	FOR USE ONLY IF EVACUATION IS CARRIED OUT										
		NUMBER ACTUALLY TAKEN				WEEKLY AMOUNT PAYABLE £ s. d.	ADDITIONAL BEDDING ISSUED				REF. TO ROLL OF TAXED PERSONS IN DWELLING
		CHILDREN		NO. OF ADULTS AT 5/-	NO. OF CHILDREN (NOT BOARDED) AT 3/-	OTHERS AT		MATTRESSES		BLANKETS		
		NO. OF UN-ACCOMPANIED CHILDREN AT 10/6	NO. OF UN-ACCOMPANIED CHILDREN AT 8/6					DOUBLE	SINGLE	DOUBLE	SINGLE	
H. T. G. Gleave Esq												
Mr E. Hall	unea case : of nursing											
Mrs E. Bristow	very delicate could not look after children											
Mr A. Bristow Junr	boys preferred											
Mr A. Bristow Senr	girl preferred											
Mr H. H. Young	objects to evacuation scheme											
Capt Jenkins	let at week end lone only											
Mr B. J. Cook	Post Office & business Premises, unable to take any one											
Mr A. D. Leslie												
Mr A. D. Leslie												
Mr D. Dann	unable to take children through old age & infirmity											
Mr Tidy												
Mr V. Marsh	not willing											
Mr J. Marsh	Mrs Marsh would prefer to join up for other work											
Mrs Webb												
Sir H. Wilson	In a crisis is willing to give up the house to 6 children & 1 adult											
Mr Geering	furnished house used occasionally for week ends											
Mrs Worsdell	would prefer Rent & work											
Misses Symonds	one very delicate & unable to take children											
Mrs Hollingdale	all residents over 70											
Mrs Huntley												

All households in Chailey were assessed for their suitability to take in evacuees, and the notes in the register show a variety of responses by local people. While Sir H. Wilson 'in a crisis is willing to give up the house to six children and one adult,' Mr H. H. Young 'objects to evacuation scheme'. He was not alone: on another page Major Huggins, of Romany Ridge, 'objects very strongly to the whole scheme.'

Ditchling. October 2, 1939
It was resolved to apply for public air raid shelters with a total capacity of 300 persons.

Herstmonceux. December 5, 1939
Chairman read letter from the rural district council on the subject of National Savings, asking for the support of the council in the way of propaganda and formation of savings groups.

Burwash. January 15, 1940
'That a letter be written to the chief billeting officer that it was the opinion of the parish council that the number of evacuee children in Burwash, Burwash Weald and Burwash Common was far in excess of the capabilities of the householders, some of whom were breaking down with the strain.'

Guestling. January 16, 1940
A communication from the RDC of Battle respecting the calling of the fire brigades in emergency. It stated that 'A householder in case of fire should pick up the receiver and call "Battle Fire Brigade, fire at —", when, under present conditions, one or two engines should be in attendance within 15 minutes.'

Herstmonceux. January 16, 1940
Chairman stated that he had been informed by the clerk to the rural district council that the triennial election of parish councillors in March 1940 will not take place owing to the war — but that the present councillors will remain in office for the duration of the war.

Ticehurst. March 19, 1940
Mr Dungey brought before the council the hardship of many parishioners during the severe weather owing to the coal shortage, stating that he considered a complaint should be made to the fuel controller, asking why our local coal merchant should not be able to procure any coal while in the neighbouring village of Wadhurst the coal merchants there not only had sufficient to supply their own registered customers but to supply to all and sundry in Ticehurst.

Heathfield. March 26, 1940
The clerk read various letters from the secretary to the Heathfield and District Horticultural Society in which he forwarded the names of eight applicants for allotments.

Burwash. July 15, 1940
Mr Whitaker explained a scheme in connection with the Battle RDC for the collection of old iron, waste paper, cardboard and rags. Arrangements to be made for house to house visitation, and for people to let the council know where they might collect, and a lorry would be sent for it. Some of the metal would have to be sold to defray the expenses of the lorry.

Herstmonceux. July 16, 1940
German gun. The chairman referred to the above and gave a brief outline of its history since being in the parish. He considered that it should now be made use of as scrap.

Guestling. July 18, 1940
A communication from the RDC of Battle was received. It asked that obstructions should be placed on large fields to prevent the landing of enemy aircraft. It also asked for voluntary labour for this purpose. The clerk was directed to reply that, after enquiries, no men were available for this purpose.

Pett. August 6, 1940
The council had before them complaints of residents as to the manner in which Government work on the defence preparations at Pett Level had been carried out. Allegations were made as to inefficiency, idleness and the employment of men unequal to this task by reason of their physical condition. Further, a lack of supervision was stated to have contributed to the deplorable position.

CIVIL DEFENCE.

Equipment supplied to Newick Civil Defence by The Newick Parish Council.

Iron Rations to value of £ 1- 11- 8 g.
1, Extending Ladder.
1, 63 ft length rope.
6, Galvanized Pails.
2, Crowbars.
1, Pickaxe.
1, Mattock.
3, Axes.
1, Axe.
2, Shovels.
21/4, Steel Helmets.
1, Pyrene Portable Fire Extinguisher.
1, do hand do do.
19, Stirrup pumps.
14, Boiler suit Overalls.

For and on behalf of Newick Civil Defence Committee.

Head Warden. L.A.R.P.

Received 12/2/42

Newick's iron rations for opposing Hitler's invading army.

Danehill. September 3, 1940
Mr Richard Chalterton, head of the local AFS, attended the meeting and spoke of the arrangements made in the village for fighting fires. He pointed out that fires were started not only by incendiary bombs, but by the effects of blast from high explosive bombs. In each case the stirrup pump was the best means of fighting such fires at the commencement. Mr Chalterton then mentioned the serious shortage of water in the parish. In fact the shortage was so acute that it would be impossible to use the fire engine at Uckfield which the AFS men had been trained to use. In view of this difficulty it was agreed to send a letter to the district council pointing out the shortage of water and the fact that, as the AFS are not full-time men, it would take some time to collect them from their homes and places of employment. Under these conditions, the council desired to ask the district council to supply a number of stirrup pumps, one for each six adjacent cottages, and one to each isolated cottage, about 100 pumps in all.

Pett. September 24, 1940
It was reported that no acknowledgement or reply had been received to the further communication addressed to the Officer Commanding troops at Pett and respecting the dangerous manner in which military transport was being driven in this and neighbouring parishes.

Ditchling. December 6, 1940
Certain roadside defence pits dug by the military authorities, but now decayed and apparently abandoned, had become a danger to the public. The clerk was instructed to bring this matter to the notice of the military authorities.

Danehill. January 29, 1941
Bomb crater in cemetery. Referring to the damage done in the cemetery by a high explosive bomb, the chairman said the council's most grateful thanks was due to Mr C. Etherton and his band of voluntary workers for restoring order out of chaos. In a letter to the council Mr Etherton wrote that the work had been completed, although it had taken them longer than anticipated. The reason for this was that about half of those who promised to help did not turn up at all.

Salehurst. January 30, 1941
Mr Chandler reported that the sum raised for the county Spitfire Fund amounted to £46.7.0. He hoped that an effort would be made to increase this to £50.

Burwash. April 21, 1941
Mr Whitaker, as chairman of War Weapons Week, gave a report to the saving campaign that Mrs Fogden did most excellent work, the result being most successful, over £8,000 being raised.

Pett. May 15, 1941
The clerk submitted a letter respecting the 'Grow-to-it' production of vegetables etc in rural areas. It was pointed out that the council owned no land in the parish and there were no vacant allotments. The council decided to call the attention of the new rector to the leaflets, with respect to the rectory grounds.

The attention of the council was drawn to an accident which had happened in Pett, in which a little girl had been injured. It was decided to ask the military authorities to caution all dispatch riders to take the utmost care when negotiating the narrow and twisting roads in the parish.

Danehill. September 30, 1941
Iron and steel railings. The clerk was instructed to inform the district council that this parish council, after making a very careful survey of the parish, regret that a schedule of railings cannot be furnished, as in the opinion of the council none could be removed other than those in use to prevent cattle from straying.

Salehurst. October 21, 1941
Memorial clock. The clerk reported that Mr A. Duck had been winding the memorial clock on behalf of Mr F. Brett who had now enlisted in the Royal Air Force. Mr Duck is willing to continue to wind the clock in this manner but would be unable to accept a direct appointment as he is a full time member of the fire brigade. The council felt that this method would be far from satisfactory, for in the case of an accident to Mr Duck the liability would fall on Mr Brett, and the council's workmen's compensation policy would be inoperative. After some discussion it was decided to make a new appointment and Mr H. Mabb was appointed to commence duties from 27th October 1941 at a remuneration of one shilling per week.

Ticehurst. November 17, 1941
Public air raid shelter. Mr Malcomson wished to state that the public shelter behind the Bell Hotel fence had two feet of water in it, and that the roof leaked.

Ditchling. December 2, 1941
The clerk reported that it having come to his notice that the barbed wire entanglement on the pathway at the junction of South Road and the Brighton Road were a source of danger to the public, especially at night, and in more than one instance had caused damage to pedestrians' clothing, he had written to the Officer Commanding the troops in Ditchling, asking for a light or white board to be put beside the obstruction as a warning.

Ditchling. February 17, 1942
War Ships Week. Dr Clifton Harris reported that Chailey rural district is to aim for a corvette, the total cost of which would be £120,000. Ditchling is to have as its particular object armaments and ammunition for the corvette. The amount aimed at for War Ships Week is £11,500, of which £2,500 is already promised.

Burwash. March 16, 1942
Complaints received respecting a shop in High Street, being painted a
bright red, with large white letters advertising 'Snack Bar', Suppers, Teas
etc was considered to be an eyesore to the village and not in conformity
with the colour of other houses (but the use of the house as a tea room
for troops was considered useful).

Herstmonceux. March 24, 1942
'We, the parish council of Herstmonceux, view with great concern the
complete absence of emergency food in the parish at the present time,
and consider that the food organiser should give the matter his immediate
attention.'

Burwash. March 26, 1942
Cllr Wuille reported that a sub-committee had been into the question
of unfair distribution of oranges, and had compiled a table in respect
to the amount of oranges distributed through the parish since May 1941.

Burwash. October 12, 1942
The clerk was instructed to write to the Battle RDC as to the unsatisfactory
state of the lavatory pans in the air raid shelters.

Danehill. November 19, 1942
A letter was read from the War Graves Commission regretting that such
cost as expenses for refreshments was not permissible as part of the
refund against the Commission.

Danehill. February 18, 1943
Invasion arrangements. The chairman read letters requesting completion
of arrangements in the parish to be put into operation in case of
emergency. The letters gave particulars of what was required from local
authorities: 1 To arrange sites for communal burial in Danehill and
Chelwood Gate; 2 To appoint a parish registrar, 3 To select suitable
buildings for mortuaries.

Herstmonceux. March 23, 1943
'That the Herstmonceux parish council is seriously concerned to find
that the central pharmaceutical war committee is contemplating closing
the only chemist's shop at Herstmonceux by transferring the proprietor
to another district. As this shop serves a number of villages in the vicinity
and no other chemist's shops are nearer than Hailsham, Sidley, Heathfield
or Horam Road, the parish council wishes to bring this fact most forcibly
to the committee.

Hellingly's sports pavilion was one of many buildings erected as war memorials.

Hartfield. May 24, 1943
The meeting was called for the purpose of asking the food controller if some arrangement could be made for the ration cards etc to be distributed locally other than at Crowborough.

Burwash. July 26, 1943
The hon sec of Burwash National Savings Council wrote that during Wings for Victory Week the parish had raised £11,371 (the target was £10,000).

Salehurst. September 9, 1943
The Rev. Ward stated that judging by the number of marriages of soldiers and other young people wishing to get married if houses were available, he thought some 36 houses would be required in Robertsbridge. After some discussion on the subject, it was finally decided to inform the RDC

THIS PAVILION
IS ERECTED IN
GRATEFUL MEMORY
OF THOSE
PARISHIONERS
OF HELLINGLY
WHO LOST THEIR
LIVES WHILST
ON SERVICE IN
THE WORLD WAR
1939-1945

that the immediate postwar needs would be Robertsbridge 50, Hurst Green 12, the Junction 4.

Ticehurst. October 14, 1943
Post-war housing requirements: Flimwell 25 cottages (12 of them required immediately); Ticehurst 20 cottages (including two tied, 14 of these required immediately); Stonegate 13 cottages (including four tied, eight of these required immediately).

Arlington. November 3, 1943
On or about 29th October a plankway bridge at Sessingham was reported to be missing. Clerk was instructed to make a claim to the military concerned.

Ticehurst. December 9, 1943
The chairman reported that he had had a letter from the Battle RDC asking the opinion of the parish council before sanctioning a meat pie scheme in the parish of Ticehurst, and that he had approved the scheme.

Burwash. January 17, 1944
A special meeting of the council to discuss the housing of the working classes. The committee suggested that at least 24 would be required.

Arlington. April 5, 1944
Mr Marchant reports Army backed through his hedge near Sessingham Bridge and carried away another stileway. He hopes to obtain compensation from military.

Ditchling. April 18, 1944
Report of food production and allotments committee: Mr Holman reported that the membership of the Ditchling Produce Association was now 98. There would be a produce show in October.

Heathfield. April 18, 1944
Housing of the working classes. Mr Hart reported that the Minister of Health had cut down the number of cottages for the rural district, so he was afraid that the number asked for by this council, *viz* 10, would be cut accordingly.

Ditchling. July 21, 1944
The chairman reported that housewives were finding much difficulty in providing meals for the RAF personnel billeted in their houses. The hours were very awkward, and the amount of labour involved, instead of being concentrated in one mess, and so reduced to a minimum, was out of proportion to the numbers fed, which seemed wasteful. He suggested that proper messing facilities should be provided by the Air Ministry in the village.

Ticehurst. October 12, 1944
War damage. Several members complained of the amount of time wasted by the repair gangs in acquiring mushrooms, rabbits, blackberries and apples.

Salehurst. October 17, 1944
A discussion ensued on the latitude allowed to the Italian collaborators stationed at the Robertsbridge camp, there being an increasingly hostile feeling towards these men due to women being accosted after 'black out' time. It was proposed by Dr Dingley, and agreed, that letters be sent to Sir George Courthope MP and the regional commissioner pointing out the seriousness of permitting the Italians to roam about the streets and lanes until 10pm and suggesting that they should all be in the quarters not later than 7pm during the winter months.

Pett. March 16, 1945
This meeting was called to meet some representatiave inhabitants of the parish to take part in an informal discussion as to what form a war memorial should take. Proposals were made and discussed. These included: 1. The building and endowment of one or two bungalows for ex-servicemen and their families; 2. A social centre to be added to the village hall; 3. A permanent playing field invested in the village; 4. A collection of money to be added to collections from other Sussex communities to forward a large donation to Oswald Stoll Settlement for a centre to be established in Sussex for Sussex ex-service wounded men.

Ditchling. May 15, 1945
The chairman stated that more petrol must be obtained for the motor-mower if the playing field was to be brought into its pre-war state. He thought application might be made for this in view of the Prime Minister's recent announcement on the subject.

Hartfield. July 13, 1945
Removal of barbed wire. The clerk was instructed to write to the East Grinstead UDC, asking if it had any suitable place where this could be dumped.

Heathfield. September 4, 1945
Victory celebrations. After some long discussion it was eventually agreed that sports and a tea should be held for all the children from ages 3 to 14 who attended either Broad Oak, Old Heathfield, Punnetts Town, Vines Cross or Maynards Green schools, and others living in the parish of Heathfield.

Arlington. October 3, 1945
Resolved that the war agricultural committee be informed that, in view of the fact that grazing rights are held, that the condition of the Milton Hide after occupation by the military requires looking into.

Danehill. December 13, 1945
Dane Hill Cricket and Football Clubs. 'Sir, your letter of the 2nd instant regarding the Dane Hill playing field was placed before the last meeting of the executive committee. Each case must be considered on its merits, and in the case of the above field the committee have recommended the Ministry that the land should be reseeded as soon as the present growing crop has been harvested.'

Ditchling. April 16, 1946
A letter was read from the clerk to the Chailey RDC about 28 × 2lb tins of guava jelly given by the inhabitants of South Africa for distribution to the aged and needy people in the Ditchling parish.

Danehill. June 6, 1946
The clerk was directed to arrange with the district council for the removal of all war-time roadside emergency obstructions at Freshfield Lane, Church Road, and the filling-in of gun site pits and trenches at the junction of Sandy Lane and Lewes Road, Chelwood Gate.

Burwash. July 3, 1946
The clerk produced a letter from the Prime Minister on food waste. This was read, and passed on to Cllr Miss Parker, with a view to her placing it before the Women's Institute.

THE CLERK'S TALE

An essential ingredient of any successful parish council has always been an apparently all-seeing, all-knowing and meticulously efficient clerk. These lowly-paid part-timers manage the agendas, balance the books, keep the records and advise councillors on any number of technicalities — and their workload has grown considerably since the second world war as the parish councils have steadily taken on greater responsibilities. How do they themselves see their job?

Bert Crouch, born in 1900 (a mere six years after the civil parishes were created), served Hellingly parish council for a remarkable fifty years — for the first two years as a councillor and then, from 1939 to 1987, as clerk. Despite his own modest disclaimers, the title of 'Mr Hellingly' bestowed upon him by the local newspaper seems fully justified: he had an influence on every major project in the village during that half century, whether in his capacity as clerk or in his unofficial role of tireless, community-minded wheeler-dealer. The recreation ground and its pavilion, the village hall, the sports club, the most recent extension to the cemetery — he was a moving force behind all of them.

❝ The job paid £35 a year when I started, and you didn't get any training whatsoever. It's not much more than a thousand pounds now, so you still do it basically for love. I had to learn the hard way, and I obviously made a few mistakes from time to time, but I did make a study of local government because I thought that was important. I took a course, and passed the examination.

You do need a head for figures. That was something I was very strict on. You went to the district audit, you see, and I didn't want any trouble with them. they were very, very tight. It's your reputation when it comes to the audit, and I didn't want to soil mine.

Until the 1972 Act you were severely limited in what you could spend as a council. A fourpenny rate, I think it was. If you wanted more than that, you had to go to the parish meeting. Parish councils in those days

45

wouldn't spend a farthing. They were very tight: they honed everything down.

But in those days nearly everybody had their roots in the parish. That died eventually, with the newcomers taking over. I doubt if you've got anyone on the parish council at all now that has any roots, that can look back many years as a resident. Of course this has brought in some new ideas, but I think it's a loss, nevertheless. Those old folk knew what was good for the parish.

Meeting the people was one of the things I most liked about the job, and knowing everyone was very useful. It was a parish of wide open fields then, not developed as it is now. You got to hear what was going on, and you were able to do your bit to help. That's how I saw the job: I worked with the council for what I considered the good of the parish. I was interested in Hellingly and I wanted to see it grow.

During the war I was in charge of National Savings for Hellingly, and eventually for the whole district. We raised £88,000 by organising fetes, whist drives and concert parties. There'd be special savings weeks — Salute the Soldier, Wings for Victory. Each parish had a target, and we reached it every time. I was invited up to Buckingham Palace afterwards, in recognition of what I'd done.

Apart from organising everything, I'd attend every event and make a speech.

Hellingly's scout hut, Crouch Hall, honours the parish's long-serving clerk.

Whip it up a bit! I remember getting the RAF Central Dance Band down here. The RAF had a depot at Wartling. I knew the people there, and they did it for me.

Having your ear to the ground was very important. During the 1960s we had a chance to buy the village hall, which we'd rented since 1914. It was talking to people in the know that prompted me to put in an offer of £2,000 on the council's behalf. When I tell you that we immediately insured it for £10,000, you'll see that it was a bit of a bargain.

But don't get the idea that this was in any way a one man show. A village like Hellingly thrives on its volunteers. After we bought the Lower Horsebridge recreation ground in the early Fifties we built the pavilion entirely with voluntary labour. I'm not sure that you'd get that spirit now.

Mind you, in Hellingly we always had quite a bit of interest from the residents. We'd have twenty or thirty turning up to most meetings. The important thing is to get notice of the meeting printed and distributed about the parish, and then to get the councillors to nudge people to come along.

Party politics have come into it a bit during the last few years. I don't like that. It used to be that everybody was working for the benefit of the parish rather than for a party. It's not the same, in my opinion.

The job of clerk has grown steadily busier over the years. There's quite a bit of paperwork, and Hellingly is one of the biggest parishes with more services than most. We've the recreation ground and the cemetery, and I had as many as 72 footpaths to look after when I was there. When I left, they split the job up because it had grown so big.

Clerks get a proper training now, I'm pleased to say, but there's still nothing like experience. Because I'd been doing the job so long, I was always being asked for advice.

I remember a fellow clerk coming to me very worried because there'd been a terrible mix-up at the churchyard, and the wrong body had been buried there. What could he do?

Well, I knew the answer to that, because I'd had the same embarrassing problem some years before. One poor woman had visited the mortuary to identify her mother's body, only to discover that it was someone else altogether. Her mother was already under the ground at Hellingly, when she was actually supposed to be buried in another parish.

What you do is get special authority from the bishop, and that isn't cheap. Then a large coffin has to be made and the existing coffin raised and put inside it. And one more thing — you have to carry out the operation at first light. **9**

Paula Fisher has never had to keep a graveside vigil at dawn, but as the clerk to Battle town council she has rather more responsibilities than the average parish clerk. Like many a local public servant, she started in a small way but very soon found herself thoroughly involved.

6 It all started in the 1970s when I answered an advertisement for a part-time job assisting the then clerk. I never envisaged that I'd be with the council anything like this length of time, but about 18 months later the clerk became

47

ill. It was a smallish enterprise then, and I took on a bit more, and then a bit more again, and when the job was eventually advertised some of the councillors asked why I didn't apply for it. I'd never thought of being anything more than a helper, but this is how it's turned out.

When I first joined we weren't even in a proper office: we used the front room of the clerk's house. Later on we found rooms in the high street which overlooked the Abbey. Now we're in the Almonry, which is one of the oldest buildings in the town and dates back to medieval times: it's a lovely place to work.

Battle has always been very much a place to do its own thing. The town council looks after the cemetery and the 'closed' churchyard. We've two recreation grounds and a 20-acre wood — the county council, through the community woodland scheme, encouraged parish councils to identify unused woodland, and as a result of this we were given Mansers Shaw. We're managing it as an open space. The council also owns 24 acres to the south of Battle Abbey, which we bought when the Abbey was sold by the Websters to the Department of the Environment.

We don't have to find money from the rates for all these things because we have quite an income. For instance, the council negotiated with the Department of the Environment to run the car park by the entrance to the Abbey. At the time visitors were allowed to park willy-nilly all over the place. It was an absolute disaster, because if you don't have lines on a car park people misuse it. We put in a bid to run it properly and they said: You can if you want to, but you'll never make any money.

Well, the chairman at that time was an accountant. He worked out every space, and a theory of how many times each one would be occupied in a day — and he was right almost to the penny when we started it off. There are only 27 spaces, but it makes about £20,000 a year.

It's always been the council's policy to have a go, to do things ourselves. Before deciding on projects like this the council calls a public meeting, and usually the people are very supportive. It's a very traditional sort of town.

Does the clerk run the council? Yes and no. I do perhaps have a tendency to jump in where angels fear to tread, and I *have* made mistakes from doing that. Inevitably you do: you just have to put things right afterwards. By and large, though, the councillors tell you what they have in mind, and your job is to find a way of doing it.

There are times, of course, when you have to take quick decisions without referring them up. The council runs forty allotments, and I well remember the time a fight broke out between two of the tenants. One had started a bonfire, which became somewhat smoky. The tenant of the adjoining plot, a rather spirited lady, asked him to put it out. When he refused, she went home, collected a bucket of water and not only put out the fire but soaked her neighbour at the same time. Both of them marched into my office — separately, thank goodness — and I had to find a way of making the peace.

I wasn't trained at the outset, but I'd been a secretary and I'd taken minutes for various organisations. In 1988 I gained a certificate in local government administration. I found the finance side perhaps a bit difficult to begin with, but now I love figures rather more than writing minutes.

As for what the job entails, I'm the chief executive of the town council. That's what parish clerks are, too — quite a responsibility, but you find that help is always at hand.

You don't work off your own bat, of course: it's governed by what the law and the council will allow you to do. After all, you have to present everything to them. To take an actual example, the council might wish to buy the Almonry. They'll ask you to get into discussions with the county council and any other relevant authority. You have to get all the facts and figures and see whether you can get a package together. You have to do the research and work out the costings.

It's difficult to analyse. If I gave you a job description with a list of all the things I do, it would make a book in itself! Officially I work for 27.75 hours a week, so that I can be free for the other things I enjoy — the women's institute, amateur dramatics, gardening, and a host of other things. In reality, I probably *do* work full-time.

The Almonry, Battle — the council's headquarters, and 'a lovely place to work'.

I have no doubt about the value of parish and town councils. Looking after your own affairs is very important. Of course a council's powers are limited, and you can't, at the end of the day, stop a road going through or a housing development being approved. In those cases it's a question of organising the troops on the ground and having a public meeting and stirring up the interest. We've a council of 17 members, and they belong to an awful lot of organisations between them. They're certainly very representative of the feeling of the town.

Councils may have more responsibilities after the next reorganisation of local government, and that would be a very good thing. I think in Battle, for example, we would very much like car parking under our control. That's something which is easily undertaken at grass-roots level.

Of course we would need more expertise to tackle some of these functions, but personally I've always had a lot of help from the higher authorities, and there are ways and means of finding out how to deal with *any* situation. It's a question of going to the right place for the right information.

Grass-roots democracy cuts through the stifling, bureaucratic paraphernalia. It keeps people happier. **9**

Robin Symington *co-founded* The Living World *exhibition at the Seven Sisters Country Park, eventually selling it so that he could spend more time at home in Chiddingly with his young family. It was because of his close involvement with the community that when, in 1989, it was suggested that he apply for the post of parish clerk, he found the proposition impossible to refuse.*

6 One of the things I was doing after selling the exhibition was offering to do typing and word-processing, because I had computer equipment at home. I typed quite a lot of correspondence for the chairman of the parish council, who I knew, and I ended up typing so many letters that he encouraged me to go the whole hog. The clerk at that time lived outside the parish, and it was difficult to get in touch with him. The chairman pointed out that I was on the doorstep and had all the equipment: what could be more logical?

I'd known a previous clerk, and I'd seen advertisements for a clerk in the parish magazine. They more or less said that no experience was necessary, only a knowledge of the parish and a willingness to work long hours for miserable pay! I thought that I'd been doing that for a number of years in any case, so I applied and was voted in.

People probably imagine a clerk to be someone pottering away with a typewriter and taking a few minutes, pushing out a few letters and being a bit interfering at times. I don't think they see it as much more than that, but in fact there's so much more to be done these days — so many more planning issues especially. This is the most important work in a small parish.

East Sussex is a very crowded area. All land is under pressure and most of it is conserved or preserved in some way or another. That means that the job isn't just a matter of recording some minutes or writing off a few letters. There's an element of diplomacy and an element of knowledge of the community, and equally these days you need to be quite sharp on planning legislation — what's allowed and what isn't, what's in the county structure plan and so on.

I get the structure plan and the district plan as they come out. Wealden District Council and the Sussex Rural Community Council hold meetings for clerks, and I go to all of those. That's how I try to keep up to date.

As clerk I ought to hold no opinion. A clerk really is a one-man civil service. He's the paid officer, and his job is to carry out the wishes of the council. You can certainly have private conversations outside of meetings, and perhaps try and either form an opinion or influence opinion and offer advice, but at the end of the day the clerk has no vote and no say.

Of course it's tempting to get involved, but if it was a planning issue I'd be very wary because there are financial implications. You can't personally interfere — stop somebody carrying out a development, say, or demolishing something or cutting down a tree. That doesn't go down at all well. It doesn't do to encroach upon people's private lives, and I'd fight shy of that.

But if it were a matter of the provision of facilities for, say, school children, or for the village as a whole — things that there would appear to be a consensus on, like maintaining a village hall, school playing fields, bus shelters, keeping pavements in good repair, the sort of basic facilities and amenities of a community — then I don't see any harm in interfering to improve those.

The necessary attributes of a clerk? I suppose one obviously should be able to get on with people. I don't know whether I fall into that category or not, but a willingness to cope with all sorts of people in all sorts of situations is necessary. It helps a great deal if you live in the community. That's what I think, although a lot of clerks say it's an advantage to live outside, because they can be neutral and dispassionate. I wouldn't agree at all. I think if you know the people in your community, and what they're about and the way they work, you can possibly see awkward situations arising and stop them before they happen. That's so much better than having to march in after something awful has happened and trying to sort it out later.

You can see the way things are going in your village: the closure of a church or a shop or a pub. That's happening all over the place nowadays, and if you live in a community you can see what's happening to all the basics of English rural life in your own patch, and perhaps step in before it's too late.

I love the work. It's a much more rewarding and interesting job than I could ever wish for, because it's not all about business and promotion and making money, but about looking after and maintaining — and perhaps improving — a community. I've got children who live in that community, and it's nice to think that one may just be maintaining or improving it in some way for them to inherit.

The voluntary sector — I'd almost call it that because of the pay — has a lot going for it, in my opinion. Our community happens to be a thriving one, a happy one, a close-knit one and a friendly one. I'm dead lucky. Chiddingly is a very active village. We have a festival, three flower shows (I think we're one of the six villages in England that have three flower shows a year), three lively pubs, two thriving shops, a church that's open and active, a school with bigger numbers than it's had for some considerable time and a village hall. Now there's talk of a new school sports hall going up.

I've been a clerk for only a few years, but I suspect that there's a greater exercise of grass-roots democracy today than ever before. The pace of life is so much quicker and with modern communications you can find out what people want more quickly and pass that on. People equally, these days, are so much more aware of their rights. They're more aware of what other people are doing, and they're much more ready to say 'we want that, too'. There are a lot more voices rising up from the general public.

Parish councils, because they're at the grass roots, because they're in a community, and because parish councillors have to face the people who vote for them and whose planning applications they're considering, do have an important role representing what local opinion is all about. I do feel fairly passionate about that

We have very little statutory or legislative power, but what we do have is 'people power'. There may be only 650 adults on the Chiddingly electoral roll, but if there's a contentious issue about which everyone in the parish is agreed, a parish council can help to focus and coordinate both opinion and action. Fuelled by the people power of 650 united raised voices a parish council can be a formidable opponent.

But a parish councilf isn't really here to say 'Thou shalt not!', even if that may sometimes be necessary. It's here primarily to be helpful and constructive; to be a force for the improvement of the community.

My job as clerk is to try to make this a reality. **,**

OF PONDS AND CLOCKS AND THE VILLAGE STOCKS

The most effective riposte to claims that parish councils do nothing and know nothing is to furnish the critic with a list of their potential responsibilities — the kind of list, indeed, which appears in the leaflet reproduced on the following two pages. The smaller parishes may choose to wield very few of their powers, whereas the towns will use most of them, but these mere minnows in the shark-infested political waters nevertheless graze an impressively wide territory.

This chapter, being a brief photographic essay, inevitably fails to do full justice to such an abundance of interests. By necessarily concentrating on objects, it perhaps gives undue weight to those things which the councils have inherited (the clocks and village stocks of the title, not to speak of the macabre skull at Rye town hall), at the expense of the many amenities they are currently providing. Commons, playing fields and car parks rarely lend themselves to this kind of snapshot treatment, and village halls are so widespread that it would be invidious to select only two or three. Some highly commendable facilities (the mini recycling plant for paper, plastic and cans in Plumpton's playing field, for instance) are apt to look merely comical before the camera's stern gaze.

Also missing, inevitably, are intangible benefits such as bus pass and concessionary fare schemes. These are often financed by the raising of 'the free two pence' — the maximum rate local councils are allowed to spend each year on services not included on their standard agenda.

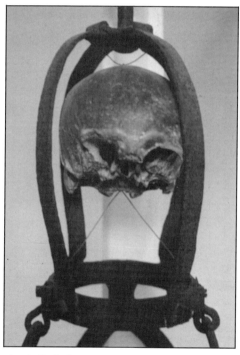

The skull of John Breeds, hanged for murder at Rye in 1742, is perhaps the most bizarre of all the artefacts inherited and preserved by our local councils.

Even allowing for these omissions, however, our humble black-and-white exhibition surely establishes a simple truth: that the activities of a lively parish (or town) council will touch our lives at every turn.

The National Association of Local Councils

(representing Parish, Town and Community Councils)

108 Great Russell Street, London, WC1B 3LD

What Can Local Councils Do?

(A summary of their powers for those who want better villages and towns)

The powers which have been vested in Parish, Town and Community Councils by Acts of Parliament are summarised in this leaflet as a guide to Councillors and others. Each description is brief and is intended to be a general indication. Like all powers given to public bodies the powers of local councils are defined in detail in legislation and these details may include a requirement to obtain the consent of another body (for example the approval of the County Council to the provision of a car park). Local Councils must exercise their powers also subject to the provisions of the general law (for example planning permission is necessary for a sports pavilion). Information on all these details should be in the hands of the Clerks of the Councils. The standard text-book, *Local Council Administration* by Charles Arnold-Baker, which is sold by the Association, is the complete guide to the powers and functions of local councils.

The powers are listed alphabetically. Where a power is marked with an asterisk the council may, in addition to exercising the power itself, help another body to act by giving financial assistance.

Allotments Provision and maintenance of allotments for cultivation.

*Arts Developing and improving knowledge of the arts and the crafts which serve the arts.

Baths Provision of baths and wash-houses (which in modern terms may mean a launderette).

*Cemeteries Provision and maintenance of burial grounds, or cemeteries, or crematoria.

Churchyards Power to contribute to the costs of a churchyard in use and a duty to maintain any closed churchyard where the duty has been transferred by the Church.

*Clocks Provision and maintenance of public clocks, on churches or elsewhere.

Commons Power to protect any finally registered common which has no registered owner.

*Entertainments Provision of any form of public entertainment and any premises for giving entertainments. (This includes maintaining bands or orchestras and providing for dancing.)

Footpaths Maintenance of public footpaths and bridleways.

*Halls Provision of buildings for public meetings and functions, for indoor sports or physical recreation, or for the use of clubs or societies having recreational, social or athletic objects.

Legal Proceedings Power to prosecute and defend any legal proceedings in the interests of the inhabitants. Power to take part in any public local inquiry.

Lighting Provision and maintenance of any *footway* lighting which lights roads or pavements provided the columns are not above specified heights.

Litter Provision of litter-bins in streets and support for anti-litter campaigns.

Mortuaries Provision of mortuaries and post mortem rooms.

Open Spaces Provision and maintenance of public open spaces, pleasure grounds and public walks.

Parking Places Provision and management of car and cycle parks.

Parks Provision and maintenance of public parks and appropriate facilities.

Planning Local councils have a right to be notified of any planning application affecting their area and to make comments which the planning authority must take into account.

Playing Fields Provision and maintenance of land for any kind of outdoor recreation, including boating pools.

Ponds Power to deal with ponds, pools, or other places containing filth or matter prejudicial to health.

Post and Telephone Power to guarantee the postal or telephone authorities against a loss on a facility.

Public Lavatories Provision and maintenance of public lavatories.

Roadside Verges Power to plant and maintain roadside verges.

Seats Provision and maintenance of public seats on the highway.

Shelters Provision and maintenance of shelters for general public use and also particularly for bus passengers.

Signs Power to erect signs which warn of dangers or announce a place name, or indicate a bus stop.

Swimming Provision of indoor or outdoor swimming pools or bathing places.

Tourism Provision of facilities for conferences and encouragement of recreational and business tourism.

Village Green Powers to maintain the village or town green.

General Expenditure Power In any situation *not* covered by one of the specific powers described above a council may spend money on any purpose which in its opinion is of benefit to its area or to the inhabitants. The total expenditure by the council on all the cases under this general power must not in any financial year exceed the product of a 2p rate for the parish or town or community. (This power is often called 'The Free Two Pence'.)

DOES *YOUR* COUNCIL
EXERCISE *ALL* ITS POWERS?

VILLAGE SIGNS

These symbols of civic pride can be found throughout the county, and it is presumably only cost that prevents every parish having one.

The designs are predominantly historical in inspiration, sometimes heraldic: Laughton's sign displays the buckle of the Pelham family, while the Echyngham

shield has been chosen for the village from which the family took its name.

Newick's references include the Battle of Lewes (Simon de Montfort's army camped nearby) and the former hop-growing industry, while the Barcombe sign — designed and made by council chairman Alan Cannings — alludes, among much else, to the village's inclusion in the Domesday Book.

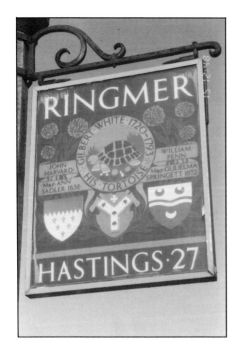

Although most of the village signs are recent, a few have graced the scene for decades.

Mayfield's which has St Dunstan and the Devil crouched beneath the nameplate, won second prize in a national newspaper competition in 1920. The chief part of the design depicts a young woman with children in a flowery meadow, a reference to the fact that the place was once known as Maid's Field.

The Ringmer sign was originally unveiled by the American ambassador in 1923, the connection being the marriages of two local women to the 17th century founders of Harvard University and Pennsylvania. (The naturalist Gilbert White often stayed in the village with his aunt, and her tortoise Timothy, in which he took a great interest, is at the centre of the composition). A replacement sign was installed in 1972: the design was identical, but the vice-chairman of the parish council lamented ('a sad reflection of the times we live in') the necessity of protecting the new one with bullet-proof glass.

RYE'S REGALIA

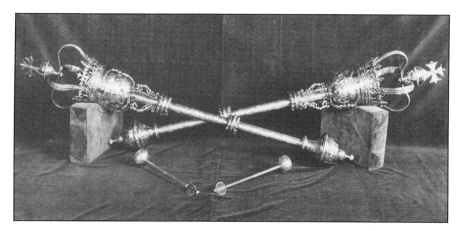

Town councils, unlike parishes, can elect mayors, but none can compare with Rye for the splendour of its historic regalia. The borough maces, which date from 1767, are made of silver gilt and weigh 986 ozs.

PEVENSEY'S 'CHARIOT'

Owning a stretch of beach is one thing: getting disabled people down to the sea is quite another. Pevensey parish council has solved the problem by installing this beach buggy (modelled for us by Cllr Hilary Marsh) at Pevensey Bay. It's known affectionately as The Chariot.

THE GREAT OUTDOORS

'Our footpaths committee chairman, Peter Royal,' writes the Maresfield clerk, 'tramps vast distances during the course of a year, accompanied by his lovely retriever, Jasper, noting where work needs to be carried out.'

Maintaining footpaths and bridleways is one of the most enthusiastically adopted powers granted to the parish councils, and a great deal of that healthy tramping takes place along the byways of East Sussex. Indeed, many councils take the responsibility of catering for their residents' recreational needs somewhat further. The walks guide published at Etchingham offers a good illustration of a council going, as it were, that extra mile.

PARISH WALKS

'Blue' Guide No.2

20p each

Highways, Bridleways & Footpaths Committee

Etchingham Parish Council

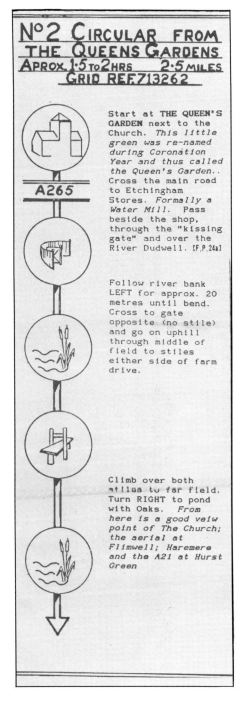

Nº2 Circular from The Queens Gardens

Aprox.1·5 to 2 hrs   2·5 miles

Grid Ref.713262

Start at THE QUEEN'S GARDEN next to the Church. *This little green was re-named during Coronation Year and thus called the Queen's Garden.*. Cross the main road to Etchingham Stores. *Formally a Water Mill.* Pass beside the shop, through the "kissing gate" and over the River Dudwell. [F,P,24a]

A265

Follow river bank LEFT for approx. 20 metres until bend. Cross to gate opposite (no stile) and go on uphill through middle of field to stiles either side of farm drive.

Climb over both stiles to far field. Turn RIGHT to pond with Oaks. *From here is a good veiw point of The Church; the aerial at Flimwell; Haremere and the A21 at Hurst Green*

The pictures on this page provide other examples: Etchingham took possession of the village pond, with plans to clean it; Pevensey bought Anderida Park, behind the castle, and built a bridge to improve access; and Long Man parish council maintains a seat at Wilmington which was presented by the widow of author Jeffery Farnol, who loved the village.

Telscombe has spent comparatively large amounts of money on maintaining open spaces. Having bought 18 acres of farmland for more than £30,000 in the early 1980s in order to create Chatsworth Park, the council paid all of £75,000 in 1989 to buy the 211 acres of Telscombe Tye, so ensuring that it would never be built upon.

Footbridge in Anderida Park, Pevensey.

Seat at Wilmington in memory of author Jeffery Farnol.

PARISH MINUTES

'About ten or twelve years ago,' reports the Pevensey parish clerk, 'the council was left a bequest, and the money was put into a trust fund for the good of the parish. The first thing it was used for was a large clock, sited on the Midland Bank building at Pevensey Bay.'

Other clocks have been inherited. Battle has two which were made in the town and are kept at the Almonry. One (*below, left*) was the handiwork of Robert Apps, who was born in Beckley in 1754 and came to Battle around 1790. The other is by Obadiah Body, born in Westfield about 1702 and working in Battle from 1730.

Towns obviously have more public clocks than villages do. The Lewes town clock (marking its incorporation), projects into the High Street by St Michael's church (*facing page, top*). There's another clock in the old market tower in Market Street, where the bell called Old Gabriel rings the hours.

Two Lewes clocks.

In villages the church often provides the one public timepiece. Parishes sometimes contribute to their upkeep, as at Willingdon (*right*) and Chiddingly.

CERAMIC MAPS

They'll never replace Ordnance Survey, but the villages of Burwash and Mayfield have attractive ceramic maps in their high streets — yet another facility entrusted to the care of the parish councils.

The Burwash map, given by the daughter of former residents Judge and Mrs Ellam, was designed by a local artist, Eileen Ware.

Ringmer

Sedlescombe

THE OLD PARISH PUMP

Every man in Newick was given two pints of beer for the celebration of Queen Victoria's diamond jubilee in 1897 — one of the first decisions taken by the new parish council, and probably the most popular. A more lasting commemoration was the installation of the parish pump, which still sits on the green today.

Ringmer's pump (*far left*) dates from vestry days, having been given to the parish in 1883, but it is, of course, maintained by the parish council today.

Sedlescombe's well and pump, its pillared housing dusted with snow in our picture, dates from 1900.

MERIDIAN MARKER

The Greenwich meridian passes through Peacehaven, and the town's founder, Charles Neville, had this monument raised in 1936 to commemorate the fact. A plaque records the distances from various parts of the Empire. The town council's guardianship of the monument hasn't been without its difficulties: the stone had to be moved 34ft during the 1980s because of cliff erosion.

THE VILLAGE STOCKS

Ninfield's stocks, which feature on the village sign (*page 66*), are made of iron — a legacy of an industry which flourished in the Weald from the 17th to the 19th centuries. (*See also the Burwash village sign, page 66*). It was at these stocks in 1790 that a man sold his wife for half a pint of gin.

THE PARISHES AT PLAY

'Our new children's playground, installed five years ago, required a loan of £10,000,' writes the Crowhurst parish clerk, 'and costs the council £2,000 annually for maintenance and service of the loan.'

Our photograph (*right*) shows only a small part of the Crowhurst equipment, which is far superior to the forlorn set of swings and a roundabout which was once the norm in council parks.

Times are changing for the better: Newick's playground (*below*), again only partially pictured, cost the council more than £16,000 and offers an enterprising range of activities for the children on sturdy, vandal-proof equipment.

Kingston, Salehurst and Willingdon & Jevington are among other parish councils which entered the centenary year with new play equipment.

Newick fishmonger.

Southdown Hunt, Newick.

POSTCARD VIEWS

One of the last things you'd expect to find in a parish council's inventory of possessions would be a postcard collection. But who better to entrust with such a valuable record of village life? The chairmen of Newick and Barcombe councils attended a postcard auction in Lewes during 1986 and successfully bid for collections which bring the past of their villages to life.

Barcombe Mills, 1910.

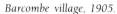
Barcombe village, 1905.

END OF THE LINE

This British Rail signal box at Uckfield was made redundant with the closure of the Lavender Line between Uckfield and Lewes. The town council bought it in 1993. 'Its future use,' says the clerk, 'has yet to be decided'.

LOOKING AFTER THE POUNDS

Nothing but a few flint walls, yet eminently worth preserving: the Long Man parish council has taken this old animal pound into its care. You'll find it close to Wilmington Priory.

THE REPORTER'S TALE

Peep through the window of the village hall while the parish council meeting is in progress and you may well find the members huddled together apparently without another soul for company. But look carefully: isn't there an isolated figure at that rickety table, scribbling away in a notebook?

This pitiable creature is a journalist. True, the inexorable retreat of broadsheet newspapers of total record before the onslaught of more scanty tabloids has brought about the virtual disappearance of the indefatigable parish pump reporter whose job it was to tour the patch covering several meetings a month, come rain, come winter darkness. Today the scribe is likely to be a keen amateur who includes parish council news among a smattering of other events when penning a few weekly paragraphs about his or her village for the local paper.

These amateurs, while providing a useful service, can hardly be expected to take the broader view. By contrast, the experienced journalist who has learned grass-roots politics the hard way is an invaluable (if less than totally respectful) guide to the true ways and means of the parish councils.

John Eccles, *now senior reporter for the* Sussex Express *in Lewes, began covering parish council meetings as a trainee journalist in the early 1960s. It was, he recalls, a confusing experience.*

❛ You have to remember that all the councillors know each other very well, whereas the poor reporter, if he's a newcomer, hasn't a clue about the people, the issues or the village. They'd be debating in their broad Sussex accents, and inevitably they'd refer to some ongoing problem about the school or the churchyard without giving any background detail whatsoever. They knew it all of course. It could take you some considerable time to work out what they were driving at — and afterwards you'd have to ask as politely as you could who it was that had been doing the talking.

The classic case was at Ringmer, where the word 'tortoise' kept coming up under Matters Arising. Month after month it went on, with the odd comment to the effect that it had been put on a shelf or in the office. I realised in the end that this was a model tortoise which had been given to the council and that there was a running debate about where to put it. Someone must have thought it was appropriate because Gilbert White's tortoise, Timothy, appears on the Ringmer village sign, and once a council has been given something it's practically impossible to get rid of it. Ringmer is one of the most efficient parish councils, but they're probably still discussing that damned tortoise!

In those days it was assumed that the members were of the Conservative persuasion. Things hadn't changed much in that respect since 1894. Apart from the inevitable farmers and landowners, there might be a few working class people on the council (a woodsman, a fencer, a very small businessman, perhaps), but they all had something to cling on to. They'd only allow change if they could benefit from it. There was a new influx of council tenants at that time, but most of them were simply glad of a roof over their heads and didn't bother themselves with voting.

Parish council meetings were almost always in the evenings and in a draughty, depressing, whitewashed hall. The one at Chailey had a tin roof, and to sit through a three-hour debate with the rain hammering overhead was to be in a war situation. You couldn't understand a word. If you fouled up your report, which wasn't surprising in the circumstances, they'd be so furious that they wouldn't let you in the next time.

At Newick there was a low beam right above the press table. You'd inevitably forget about it and crack your head, and then you'd have to put up with a stream of sardonic comments from the councillors. Very amused, they were.

Heathfield and Waldron was one of the weirdest council meetings you could hope to find. They had the unique practice of allowing the audience to take part, and some of the councillors would actually be sitting among them. That meant that you never knew who was official and who was simply putting his oar in. Utter chaos! Only the clerk knew what was going on.

Most council meetings were unbelievably boring to the outsider. An exercise in meditation: I'd often see people fall asleep. Hardly anyone turned up but the odd local eccentric and some unfortunate who wanted to get in out of the rain.

I am rather cynical about the role of the parishes. I remember, to give an example of the futility of some of their discussions, a debate at Kingston in the 1980s about emergency war plans. I listened in amazement as these worthy people seriously considered whether, if a bomb dropped on the coast, they should shoot people who were fleeing into the countryside from Brighton.

There's another kind of absurdity at Beddingham with Glynde. The councillors normally meet in Glynde, but to preserve the veneer of democracy the rules say that there has to be a meeting once every year at Beddingham. What actually happens is that they stand on the pavement outside the reading room, the clerk takes thirty seconds to read the minutes to the empty air (because no members of the public have bothered to turn up) and then they all get in their cars and drive back to Glynde.

Of course the system is potentially democratic, but parish councils have no real power. Most meetings are simply occasions for nitpicking, with councillors talking for hours about a grass verge which is, in any case, owned by the highway authority. There's very little expertise on the councils, that's the problem.

And the rules often go out of the window, in my experience. The agenda can be a bit of a joke, letters will be discussed which aren't made available and the press will be turfed out without due process.

One change for the better in recent years — a result of extensive private house building with a consequent influx of incomers — is the introduction of party politics to the parishes. It's brought some passion to the debates, and there's a more sophisticated political awareness. The parishes aren't so often run by just a few people these days. **9**

Victor Briggs, who now reports for the Kent Messenger, *recalls many an East Sussex parish council meeting covered while he was on the* Kent and Sussex Courier. *Like John Eccles, he spent countless hours in chilly village halls — although not every meeting was held in such inhospitable surroundings.*

6 Mayfield was the glorious exception. The meetings were usually held in a warm classroom at St Leonards College — or the Convent, as it's more commonly known. The room overlooked the school's swimming pool, which created an interesting diversion of thought for some members during the summer evenings.

The public meeting, at which local people were allowed to have their say, was held in the grander section of the college, the Courtyard. It was the one occasion in the year when the public usually did turn up. Regular meetings were lucky if they attracted three people at most.

Most parish meetings are extremely boring to an outsider, and I doubt if there are many reporters who actually enjoy going to them. Proceedings usually start around half past seven, and I used to feel that if they couldn't get through the agenda by nine o'clock they couldn't expect people to hang around listening. I simply used to walk out. I don't suppose that made me very popular, but I wasn't prepared to hear people going on endlessly about lampposts and verges.

You have to realise that reporters in effect aren't paid for this slog — not in their own terms of reckoning, anyway. It's considered all part of the day's work, even though by the time a meeting has ended you might have done a 14-hour day.

Mayfield Convent — a superior venue for parish council meetings.

The length of the meetings largely depends on the chairman: some cut through the business swiftly while others permit members to speak for far too long. Reporters soon get to recognise the long-winded councillors.

The shortest meeting I've ever attended lasted for only three minutes. That's a rarity, of course, but it's not as outrageous as it might seem. Parish and town councils have sub-committees which have their own meetings, and it's their recommendations which are put before the full council. If they're all nodded through there may be nothing more to discuss.

I find it surprising that so many parish councillors carry on. Most of them are well-meaning citizens who want to improve or conserve what's good in their village, but it's a boring and sometimes frustrating way to pass the time.

Many first-timers *do* bow out after their initial term, because they discover that all the grandiose and radical plans they had to offer are ignored. That's the problem, as I see it. You have to applaud the general feeling of mutual endeavour that you often find on a council, but although there's endless debate about issues which matter to the local people, at the end of the day nobody really listens to them. They have a right to comment on planning matters, for instance, but those comments have very little effect.

Of course I have had some good stories from the parish councils from time to time, but they're nearly always of the negative kind. The villagers want to stop something happening, and what makes the story is the fact that their protests are bound to be ignored. **"**

Brigid Chapman has a different tale to tell altogether. She was the very first woman sub-editor on a national newspaper (the Morning Advertiser*), but she also worked for many years in East Sussex, writing for the* Evening Argus, *the* Eastbourne Gazette, *the* Kent & Sussex Courier, *the* Brighton Herald *and the* Sussex Express. *Now a freelance journalist and author, she has happy memories of covering parish councils and a positive view of their usefulness.*

" Parish councils are the basic link between the community and local authorities, and they certainly shouldn't be maligned. I became so interested in them myself that some years ago I actually applied for the job as clerk to Milton Street council. I thought that would be rather fun. I think they paid a giddy £70 a year, something like that. It was pathetic, but I went ahead nonetheless. I think they always met in somebody's house. I went across there on a dark night, and I was given an absolute grilling. I didn't get the job, and I probably wasn't really suited to it.

In my early days as a reporter I was inevitably marked down for parish council duty. The first difficulty was getting there. They didn't provide you with a car, and if you hadn't got one of your own it was a bicycle or a bus. But once you arrived you were treated very kindly. 'Oh, you've got here,' they'd exclaim. 'How clever of you!' Then the clerk would tell the councillors that they had to get on with business pretty speedily because the local newspaper reporter had to find her way back afterwards.

As a district reporter, I regarded the parish councils as the main link with my patch. You had to know everybody. You had to read the notices on the trees to get details of the parish council meetings — and you still read the trees today.

Of course there were a few tedious meetings, but there was a simple solution to that problem. I'd talk to the clerks first, make pals with them. From the reporter's point of view a friendly and cooperative clerk was worth a guinea a minute. They knew what was coming up and you'd get the tip-off, so that you wouldn't have to stay if nothing was going to happen.

They certainly met in a strange mixture of places. During the 1960s the members of Jevington parish council would turn up about once a quarter at the former village post office. This was a damp, decaying Victorian gothic cottage, and the room the council used had ivy trailing down the wall from a hole in the ceiling.

The parish clerk was Mike Jenner, the agent to the Greek millionaire who owned the Jevington stud and a great part of the village. He handled his councillors as if they were National Hunt steeplechasers, and his minutes looked like entries in the form book.

East Dean & Friston, a very smooth and efficient parish council, met in Bardolph Hall. The local drama group used it on other occasions, and sometimes the councillors would transact their business on the stage set of *The Ghost Train* or *George and Margaret*. Somewhat bizarre, that was.

The make-up of parish councils does reflect the local community. East Dean is a bit slick. It's a wealthy village and people catch the train up to London each day, whereas some of the smaller parishes have a Hardyesque feeling to them still: the people live pretty close to the land. A colleague of mine, for example, had a very happy relationship with a parish council in a shooting area of the Weald. After meetings between September and January she'd be sure of finding a brace of pheasants in the boot of her car when she got back to base.

In these small places you've only got about three farms, twenty cottages, the church and the big house. The streets are all dark. There's no street lighting — some villages don't want it anyway, or don't want to pay for it. But these very small councils are often just as capable, because they know their area equally well. They might not have the administrative expertise, perhaps, but they know what to do.

It's in the tiny parishes like Telscombe (population about 70) that you get the unexpected or unusual stories. I used to enjoy covering Telscombe. You do go back in time there, even today. There's a very rural feeling about it.

Of course you're not looking for scandal stories, although the odd one may crop up, so it's rare for there to be any ill-feeling about what you write. You trust each other, really. You try not to let them down. You've got to live with them, remember. You've got to go back next month and the month after, so if you've dropped someone in it you're not going to get another story.

By and large parish councils do their civic duty in a commonsense way. Cackle is cut, except when old Colonel A gets on his hobby horse about the bus service, or Mrs B fulminates about bonfires. They're dealing with practical problems and often come up with practical solutions.

There's a comfortable back-to-basics feel about reporting the doings of parish councils — and I won't have a word said against them! **,**

THOU SHALT NOT

'That this Meeting resolves to use every endeavour to support the Member for this Division in his endeavour to carry a Pure Beer Bill through Parliament during the ensuing Session.'

(resolution by Ewhurst parish council,
January 17, 1901)

'That this Parish Council are of the opinion that all Motor Cars passing through this village between the Udimore Mills and the Plough Inn should be restricted to a speed of not more than twelve miles an hour.'

(resolution by Udimore parish council,
October 24, 1905)

Our parish councils are no strangers to the quixotic gesture, and who can reasonably argue against pure beer and sensible motoring speeds? Who, moreover, will take issue with Telscombe town council for protecting public decency?

'Several times over the years,' writes the clerk, 'complaints have been received from local residents about the presence of nudists on the local beach. They

Telscombe's stand against nudism. The notice on the right reads: 'We hereby inform you that there is a byelaw in existence stating that "No person shall in any street or public place wilfully and indecently expose his person" and "every person who shall offend against the foregoing byelaw shall be liable on summary conviction for every such offence to a fine".'

had been using the area for years, but always kept to 'their' side of the breakwater. Recently, however, the problem began to spread — and the activities taking place were far from simple nudism. The council's solicitor was known to take his sandwiches down to the beach, and what he saw there was not conducive to a good lunch.

'We were fortunate in obtaining superb support from the local police. Our community policeman visited the site in uniform and in plain clothes. At no time did he venture forth with *no* clothes, which we thought was cheating.

'Now, with the installation of notices on the cliff top, giving an extract from a by-law, the problem seems to have been contained. The Southern Sun Club Association set the Home Office on us, but we were able to deal with the matter, and our notices are still there. The cost has been minimal, but the results appreciated by local residents.'

This account of strenuous local authority muscle-flexing is, of course, supposed to make us smile, but the perceived nuisance was certainly real to the people involved.

'There are three lakes in the village,' reports the South Heighton clerk. 'The first lake leased by the caravan park caused a public meeting to be held in 1991. A fence had been placed around the perimeter, and a gate with a padlock was placed on the entrance.

'Angry residents felt that it had been an open space for many years, to be enjoyed by the locals. Agreement was reached with the lessee, who agreed not to padlock the gate.'

At Playden the parish council saved a playing field from being sold.

'The field is an ancient charity, administered until recently by the church,' explains the clerk. 'Various proposals for its sale had arisen from a misunderstanding that the charity was redundant.

'The parish council organised a public meeting at which overwhelming support was given for the retention of the field for occasional use, and the council has now obtained representation on the trustee body.'

However much we value their provision of basic amenities, their positive initiatives, their day-to-day conserving of the ponds and clocks and village stocks, we should also pay tribute to the tough bloody-mindedness of parish councils which prompts them, just occasionally, to declare Thou Shalt Not on our behalf. They may or may not have right on their side in any particular case, but there is something warming about their stout application of the unofficial Sussex motto 'We wunt be druv'.

Burwash and Hartfield have both won tussles with the county council.

'We had a bit of a battle with the engineers,' recalls the Burwash clerk, 'about replacing some very old lime trees. Some had already died, and we asked for a replanting to mark the Queen's 40th anniversary. The county engineers said no to the idea, but in the end we got our trees. You have to be a little insistent.'

Hartfield wanted a bridle bridge across the Medway for footpath no. 36.

'The previous one disappeared years ago,' explains the clerk, 'and the county council didn't want to spend £20,000 on a new one. Well, our footpaths committee is very active, and they felt it was an important issue. We took the matter to a public enquiry, and we won.'

A far more tempestuous controversy at Hartfield concerned a plan by a member of the De La Warr family, Lady Arabella, to build three large town houses on a plot of land close to the war memorial.

'There was an outcry in the village, and the parish council and the residents formed an association to oppose the scheme. We started a fighting fund and raised quite a large sum of money for engaging a solicitor and for getting as much publicity as possible.

'The idea was dropped after a while, and a short while ago we were able to buy most of the land. There's still £1,800 left in the kitty, and we're proposing to create a public garden there.

'A battle like that really does bring people together. Quite apart from the outcome, it can be a very good thing for a parish.'

The councils have certainly shown themselves willing to resort to the courts, if needs be at considerable expense. Streat parish meeting played David to a quarry firm's Goliath. The chairman's account:

'1986 saw the start of a planning battle by the people of Streat to rid our beautiful village of hordes of 5- and 6-axle heavy goods vehicles carrying sand from Streat sandpit and waste in the other direction.

'This culminated in 1987 in two appeals to the Department of the Environment by the owners of the sandpit. We won both of them. In 1989 three further appeals were dealt with: Streat won two of them.

'In consequence, and against all the odds, we have succeeded in ridding the lane of this traffic. We had to raise over £9,000 to meet legal and professional costs — not a bad effort by 123 people.'

Ditchling fought against the building of 55 houses on the outskirts of the village, and won on appeal. Mountfield and Brightling entered the centenary year still at combined loggerheads with Southern Water over the environmental implications of plans to enlarge Darwell Reservoir. ('We've asked the Department of the Environment for a public enquiry,' says the Mountfield clerk. 'We may be small in numbers, but we're prepared to have a go.') And Telscombe, having tussled with nudists on the seafront, celebrated the happy ending (for the time being at least) of a long-running dispute over a hall in the sequestered inland village which gives the parish its name.

'In the early 1980s,' the clerk explains, 'the trustees of Gorham's Gift took away the key to the village club, leaving the club committee without any form of access to the building which had been left to the people of the village by the squire, Ambrose Gorham. In his will of 1933 provision was made for

The hall given to the villagers of Telscombe by Squire Ambrose Gorham. The parish council became involved in a long-running tussle with the Gorham's Gift trustees over its future.

the continuation of the village club.

'The trustees wanted to make the best possible use of the charity's property, and applied to turn the building into a four-bedroomed house. In 1983 the villagers turned to the town council for help, and negotiations have been carried out since then.

'Two planning applications and subsequent appeals by the trustees have failed, and we are now taking over the club building as a village hall facility for a trial period of two years.'

This robust embracing of controversy is something relatively new. During their first fifty years parish councils could on occasion be obstinate, but few would have considered riding into battle for their residents. The change, of course, has been brought about by those residents themselves: the age of deference has long gone, and they expect their voices to be heard.

At Whatlington, in April 1972, it was a question of other voices *not* being heard. The council chairman headed an action group to counter the threat of a pop festival being held in the village.

'A collection was made from every household,' recounts the clerk, 'so that we could engage a solicitor to take legal action to prevent it.

'In the event these proceedings didn't get very far, because the festival organisers saw how determined the council and the parishioners were and cancelled their plans. The remaining balance of the money collected was returned pro rata to each household by the parish council.'

84

THE COUNCILLOR'S TALE

Standing for public office can be a prestigious business at national level, but a parish councillor can never hope to attain star status. Whatever the initial motive for seeking election, this is a foot-slogging job with, it would seem, little reward save the pleasure of serving the community. Is that really enough? Why do people do it, and does it sometimes seem like a big mistake?

Bob Poplett came to Peacehaven as a boy in 1923, his family being among the first settlers to arrive in the 'garden city by the sea' planned by the developer Charles Neville. In fact it was a wasteland of dirt tracks and undeveloped plots, and the first inhabitants felt very much like pioneers in a 'wild west' frontier town. Neville was the lord of the manor with, in those early days, almost total control of the growing township. That had changed by the time Bob, a well-known builders' merchant, first served on the parish council — but he and his colleagues had to pick up the pieces of Neville's shattered dream.

❝ His word was law, because he owned everything. In the beginning you couldn't have a house unless his company put it up. That changed later on, but Charlie Neville was the power in the land for many years, and it paid you to get on with him as best you could. He was boss man.

Peacehaven had councillors almost immediately, but we were in Piddinghoe parish then. Neville supported those councillors because he knew they'd represent his views. He controlled them through coercion and by gifts. People wanted a playing field or a club house, and he'd give the ground free and a donation towards the building. They needed to have him on their side.

After a time some of the people began to fall out with him. They wanted their rights. They wanted amenities such as lavatories that flushed, electricity, water out of a tap. We didn't have those things! Peacehaven had its own council from the late 1920s, but parish councils had very few powers and very little money. They couldn't force him to do anything. Anyway, Charlie Neville's companies went into the doldrums in the 1930s, and the war finished everything off for him.

I joined the council in 1960, but I'd been involved with it since 1951. There'd been a horrible tragedy in 1949, when a little girl wandered out of her parents' garden at Roderick Avenue and fell over the cliff. It was still unfenced, you see. There was tremendous sympathy, and enough money was raised to build a fence along the cliffs four feet high and more than a mile long. I'm pleased to say that I was one of the hard core of about twenty workers who finished that job within a couple of months.

The council really was poor in those days. It didn't even own a bucket! The councillors themselves repaired the muddy side roads and erected street signs. Even twenty years ago we had no playing fields, no public seating, no bus shelters, no main drainage. The dustbins were emptied every fortnight.

You can imagine that a councillor's life was a pretty busy one. I was chairman or vice-chairman of every committee at one time or another. During one week I attended eight meetings, including two on a Saturday and another on a Sunday. I can also remember being the only person to turn up to one meeting, which obviously had to be abandoned.

We had some unusual places for our meetings. At one time or another we met at the Peacehaven Hotel, the Central Club and the Dewdrop Inn — though not, of course, in the licensed areas. Perhaps the worst venue was the British Legion hut, where the light would go out because of power cuts, there were cold concrete floors and we had to wear overcoats to keep warm. To sort out some planning issue or other, we even met on the foreshore in a snowstorm.

The parish clerk in those days was Bill Bishop, whose equipment consisted of a pen, pencil and notepad, plus a jelly tray and wooden roller with which to print the minutes. I myself supplied the first official office for the council — above our shop. When we first employed staff to look after the sports ground we had no tractor, no gang mowers, no rollers or heavy trailers. I supplied all of those.

I was also proud to present the council, during the 1970s — by which time we'd become a town council — with the mayor's golden badge of office. We were still, as a council, poverty stricken. The mayor certainly wasn't attired as such. He was simply called 'chairman of the council'.

We've always suffered from a lack of assets, but we've come a long way since those days. Today we have a stake in Meridian Hall, offices, sports ground, sports hall, annexe hall, numerous leisure sites, the Oval, the Dell, promenade shelters, bus shelters, many public seats, playing equipment, machinery depots, Land Rover, tractors and a large amount of equipment.

In my experience the work of a councillor does take a lot of time, although you always find that some members want to get more involved than others. It's better if you've got a little business behind you that can be run without you being present. If you're employed by somebody else you tend to jeopardise your job. You have to put the job first or you may well become an *unemployed* councillor.

The rewards are a bit like those of parenthood. I used to go up and down this village feeling like an old hen looking after her chicks. I'd make a note of a sign missing here and a hole over there. You'd endeavour to get something done about it, or you'd do it yourself — and that meant going out at odd times, sometimes after dark, and to some odd places.

You know what's going on. You know before the newspapers do, and before Tom, Dick and Harry do, and you try to influence a final decision that you think will be better for a majority of the people.

The parishes may not have many powers, but often they're the connecting link between the higher authority and the people who pay the rates. It gives a bit of comfort if someone can come and talk to you.

Not that you always agree with a complaint or a campaign. Often I'd get someone say to me: 'What are we going to do about this?' and you had to weigh it up: was it beneficial to the majority or just a storm in a teacup that would blow over very quickly if you ignored it? Of course, if you didn't do anything about it you'd get yourself a slightly bad name, but if you were acting for the overall good of the community, so be it.

I retired in 1991, and I *have* missed it a little. But I'm getting on a bit now, and there were many times in the past few years when I would have much preferred not to go out when it was pouring with rain or freezing.

That's part of the job *I don't* miss!

Gail Amies *originally became a parish councillor at Salehurst in order to pursue a campaign by the community association, which she chaired, for a village hall in Robertsbridge. She later served on various council committees until, in 1983, she became chairman.*

❜ We'd formed a committee to see whether we could raise enough money to get the village hall project off the ground, and we really felt that we needed representation on the parish council if we were going to push it through. Two or three of us stood at the next elections, and I was voted in. That must have been around 1976.

I'm not at all uneasy about my motives — seeking a council place to promote a kind of vested interest. We've a population of about two thousand people here, and we were probably the only village in the area that didn't have a central meeting place. It was desperately needed. And it would, of course, be available to everybody, not a particular club or society. The campaigners were expressing the views of a large section of the village.

Once I was on the council I served my time on the various committees — dealing with footpaths, street-lighting, planning and so on. There was much more work than I'd envisaged. It's always the same when you get involved with something, isn't it?

As a member of the public you see only the tip of the iceberg. They attend our meetings, and we're fortunate that we usually do get an audience of twenty or thirty, but I think they're only seeing a slice of the work. They don't see all the committees, the site visits, the walking of the footpaths and the checking of the street lights late at night.

But being a councillor is fairly compulsive, especially if you enjoy talking to people. You make friends very quickly.

And enemies? Oh, certainly! If you have a disagreement with somebody over a planning application, for instance, some people take it very personally. I find that quite difficult, because I don't enjoy being on bad terms with people and in a village of this size it can be uncomfortable. But it doesn't happen that often. Most people are reasonable, aren't they?

That raises the question, I suppose, of what powers a parish council has. Critics either say that we have no clout at all or, if they don't like what we're doing, that we're interfering, obstructive and the rest of it.

We do have the power to precept for money, to spend as we see fit for the good of the village. We've recently taken a loan of £20,000 in order to upgrade and refurbish our children's playing area. The equipment was getting old. There were safety regulations to be taken into consideration, and there's new legislation coming in about safety surfacing under children's equipment. There were some doubts as to whether our grass surface would suffice. Quite a lot of that £20,000 has gone on safety features, but I think we've got a very attractive play area there now, and it's certainly being greatly used.

But one thing leads to another. Young mums complained to us about dogs going in there, so we've had to get a bye-law to keep them out of that particular fenced-off area.

You do learn a lot all the time, and that adds to the interest of being a councillor. But there are things that seem to run on and on for ever, too. The street light saga extends back as far as I can remember. They always seem to be either on 24 hours a day, or off 24 hours a day, and this is a source of frustration to us because we pay quite a lot of money for our street lighting.

Local councillors are very close to the grass-roots, aren't they? They're local people who talk to local people, and so a parish council ought to be expressing the views of a large section of the people who live there. You have to hope that what they think, what they pick up as they talk to their friends and acquaintances, will give them an accurate picture of what people want. I don't think that this parish council often goes out on a limb and makes a decision that horrifies most of the village.

There are controversial decisions occasionally, of course. We're having a discussion at the moment about parking in the high street — should it be restricted or should there be a free-for-all? The answer you get depends on who you're talking to at any given moment. The shopkeepers wanted an experiment of having virtually no restrictions, and that's what we're having for six months. This will be difficult, and it will be impossible to please everyone.

As chairman, my job is to run meetings reasonably professionally so that all the councillors have the chance to air their views calmly before a decision is taken. I also represent Salehurst on certain formal occasions.

Being chairman has increased my workload to some extent — when we had a public enquiry into the bypass, for instance. That was of such tremendous consequence to the village that we had to get it right. There couldn't be any messing about at a public enquiry. You had to do it properly, and that involved a lot of work.

We were in favour of the bypass, but we took issue with certain comparatively minor points. We wanted a footbridge where the bypass cut off the end of Fair Lane. We've got a small hamlet of people on the other side who weren't going to be able to walk into the village without taking their lives into their hands. And we fought hard at the southern junction where they had intended to knock down all the houses, including a pair of semi-detached cottages near Poppinghole Lane. There was a lady who had lived there all her life, and she was very distressed at the thought of having to move. We thought that it shouldn't be beyond the wit of man to devise some way of making a bypass that skirted those cottages.

At the public enquiry you had to put your evidence in written form, and then be prepared to be cross-examined by the Department of Trnsport. Your evidence was effectively disregarded if you were unwilling to submit yourself to questioning. The potential for making a fool of yourself in those circumstances is enormous, so you really have to do your homework.

I remember a barrister from the Department of Transport standing up and saying to me: 'Mrs Amies, you said a footbridge was important. Did you mean important, or very important or extremely important?'

Well, what did I mean! I had to swiftly remind myself that I was representing the parish council. I myself might find it to be absolutely vital, because I live near to it, but did everybody else feel the same way? There was no time for subtle considerations, though. I think I said 'very important', but I was so shell-shocked and frozen that I can't be sure.

We got our footbridge, and we also got the southern junction slightly realigned. That was a major breakthrough really, because we saved that lady's house. To us it was significant that in Robertsbridge the individual still mattered.

Mind you, the Department of Transport were wonderful. When I came away from giving my evidence there was a chap at the side of me saying 'Draw what you mean here.' It was literally sketched on the back of an envelope, and when I went back to the enquiry next morning the whole thing had been drawn in full detail with Parish Council Southern Junction Preferred Route printed at the top. They must have been up half the night doing that!

People laugh at parish councils, and we are a bit like Dad's Army, aren't we? There are moments in our council meetings when you can see that the public think we're creasingly funny. But that's not important — not if the council is functioning properly when it comes to the things that really matter.

My advice to anyone wanting to become a councillor is to become involved in the community first. You must get to know people. They won't vote for someone they've never heard of. I was viewed with suspicion for some time because I've only lived here since 1970, and in Robertsbridge terms I hadn't been here very long when I stood for the council. My ace card, apart from my work on the village hall committee, was that my husband's family had been here for generations, so that the name was known.

You also need plenty of spare time, although I think it's important that parish council's aren't made up entirely of retired people. That's a danger.

I've got a full-time job, and my council work is therefore of necessity done of an evening or at the weekend.

The would-be councillor should also understand that there are no allowances. Petrol, telephone, stamps — it does cost you money.

Looking ahead to the planned shake-up of local government, Salehurst would certainly hope to be given some extra powers. We'd like to have more say over minor planning matters, for instance. We've been told that major decisions can't be left to the parishes because we don't have the overview or the technical know-how which the planning authority has, but we don't see why we shouldn't deal with little extensions, porches and garages. We'd also like to handle things like repairs to footpaths, general maintenance of grass verges, grass-cutting and so on.

Parish councils have been called 'the village parliaments', and that's what they should be. People tend to come to parish council meetings to complain about something which affects them personally. Our twenty to thirty regulars who come along just to listen tend to be the same people every time. They've a general interest in what's going on. If we get sixty, then I know that thirty of them are here for a purpose! It may be a not-in-my-back-yard issue that's brought them along, and they've every right to make their protest, but the council then has the difficult task of reaching decisions which reflect a majority view.

For this reason, I think it's disappointing if you get only nine nominations for nine seats when the elections come round. You don't feel that the village has voted positively and said that these are the people they want. I'm quite happy to continue for a little while yet myself, but a challenge and a change is very healthy for democracy. **9**

John Cornwell, *a councillor for Barcombe, comes from a family with a remarkable record in parish affairs. His grandfather, Francis, who farmed the land which the Cornwells still farm today, was among the founder members of Barcombe council in 1894 and served for all of 51 years. His father, Luther, immediately took up the reins when Francis retired: indeed, he was a member not only of the parish council (from 1946-52), but of both Chailey Rural District and the county council. John became a parish councillor in 1956, which means that there was a gap of less than four years in what would otherwise have been unbroken family service since the parish councils were inaugurated.*

6 I have to say that I didn't need to do much thinking about standing for the parish council. I'd been married three years and had two very young children, but the way my father put it to me I didn't feel that I had much option. It was understood that I'd do it.

Raising a young family can be distracting, of course. My wife was pushing the pram through the village one morning when, to her surprise, she was accosted by the clerk, a retired schoolmaster. He had no hesitation in venting his stern disapproval of the fact that I had actually forgotten the first meeting I was supposed to attend!

If you ask whether there's any self-interest in standing, I'd answer in this way: I'm a farmer, and I think a rural parish like Barcombe needs to understand the farming point of view. That's useful for me, no doubt, but it's important for the village, too.

To give an example, someone coming in from the town might not be happy about some of the sights, sounds and smells of the country. Muck-spreading can be fairly overpowering if you're not used to it. The point is that it's an essential part of agriculture, and someone like me can explain why it has to be done.

As for how useful I can be, I must point out that I'm a district councillor, too. I think that's a good thing. It means that we in Barcombe are properly represented at the next level of local government, and it also means that I can report back to the parish about all sorts of things which might affect us.

Three generations of parish councillors spanning a hundred years. Francis Cornwell was elected to the very first Barcombe council in 1894 and served for 51 years; his son Luther followed him in 1946; while his grandson John was a member of the parish council in the centenary year.

Francis Cornwell

Luther Cornwell

John Cornwell

I know that people think the parishes have few real powers, but I'm convinced that we have a vital role to play. I work in this area, which is one great advantage. I've only got to cross the village street and someone nobbles me about some issue or other. I know the people and their concerns in the way that an outsider wouldn't.

All planning applications have to come before the parish for comment these days. That wasn't the case before 1974. We don't always get our way, but our views are at least registered.

If parish councils didn't exist all sorts of amenities wouldn't have been provided. I'm thinking now of the car park at Barcombe Mills which I was involved with: I went along to see the landowner, and everything moved on well from that point. Now there's a sports hall in the offing, the facilities to be shared with the primary school. Only local initiative would have brought projects like these to fruition. The fact is that the councils encourage a lot of voluntary work which otherwise simply wouldn't get done.

And we're the first to alert the higher authorities to things that need doing: a hole in the road that needs repair, for instance, or even a discreet contravention of planning law. Who else is going to notice it?

During the last decade we've certainly had more to do as councillors. Partly, I think, that's because we didn't realise what possibilities there were. Our clerk went on a course, and when he came back he put the organisation of the parish in order. Our meetings were better conducted, and we set up committees to deal with planning, footpaths, finance and so on, to ensure that the issues involved were properly considered. It had been rather haphazard before.

It's difficult to assess my parish workload because of my involvement with the two councils, but the parish alone has ten full meetings a year plus regular committee meetings. And they're longer than they used to be, too. That no doubt makes them boring to the average villager, and we certainly don't get many members of the public there.

Having said that, the parish is much more lively these days. More people are taking an interest in running village affairs. A community does need new blood, and the people who have come in have integrated quite well — joining the Barcombe Players, the Parent and Teachers Association, the Footpaths Association and things like that.

But I'm afraid that newcomers have to wait quite a long time before they can hope to get on to the council. There are only eleven places, and the long-time residents are pretty well entrenched.

I've no thought of retiring at the moment, but I suppose that when the time comes one of my sons will take the parish work on. Two of them farm with me here. We don't talk about it, but I think it's understood — just in the way it was with me and my father.

We do have a rather special tradition to keep up, after all.

EPILOGUE

The parish councils enter their second century in remarkably good heart, with a buoyancy which would have been regarded as quite unjustified only a short time ago.

There is no doubting, of course, their impressive maturing over the years: the tales unfolded here reveal how much more involved our local councils have become in the day-to-day life of their communities, what a range of responsibilities they have taken on and how a new-found confidence has seen them entering the courts to protect their people's rights.

Countering this expansive mood, however, has been a persistent assault, initiated by Margaret Thatcher and intensified by successive Conservative governments, on the scope of local democracy. Rate-capping, while it earns applause from those eager to keep costs down as a first priority, has severely limited the ability of the county and district councils to make their own decisions. Whitehall controls much more than it ever did.

As the parishes enter their centenary year, John Major's administration is pursuing plans to do away with the top layers of local government, replacing the counties and districts with so-called 'unitary' authorities. Whatever the underlying philosophy of this reorganisation — whether or not it will give the local any stronger a voice against the national — the news for the parishes (the only authorities guaranteed to emerge unscathed from the changes) appears to be very good.

'It seems unlikely that we shall be granted additional statutory powers,' concedes Dr Alex MacGillivray, chairman of the Sussex Association of Local Councils, 'yet the Government wishes to retain our contribution to local government to the extent of allowing an enhancement of our roles.'

Indeed, the new local authorities are being encouraged by Whitehall not only to consult the parishes, but actually to delegate to them some of the functions which are currently performed by the district and county councils.

For Dr MacGillivray the message is both clear and optimistic: 'The current review of local government presents our member councils with the only opportunity for some years to accept greater responsibilities.

'If the district and county councils in Sussex are replaced by several unitary authorities the representation of the people may fall well below their present levels, leaving parish and town councils to fill the gap.

'For too long we have complained that our activities — even our very existence — have often gone unrecognised in the wider world. Perhaps it is appropriate that the year in which we celebrate our centenary may also contain the means to redress the balance. We should accept the challenges these changes bring with enthusiasm.'

Certainly Dr MacGillivray has no truck with G. F. Chambers' 1894 view of parish councils as having very little to do.

'Winston Churchill said that democracy was the worst form of government except for all the others that had been tried. Well, parish councils have been tried for a hundred years. We have a good record and a bright future.

'Long live parish councils — and more muscle to their arms!'

[56 & 57 Vict.]   *Local Government Act,* 1894.   [Ch. 73.]-

CHAPTER 73.

An Act to make further provision for Local Government in A.D. 1894. England and Wales.   *15th March 1894*

BE it enacted by the Queen's most Excellent Majesty, by and with the advice and consent of the Lords Spiritual and Temporal, and Commons, in this present Parliament assembled, and by the authority of the same, as follows:

PART I.

Parish Meetings and Parish Councils.

Constitution of Parish Meetings and Parish Councils.

1.—(1.) There shall be a parish meeting for every rural parish, and there shall be a parish council for every rural parish which has a population of three hundred or upwards: Provided that an order of the county council in pursuance of Part III. of this Act—

Part I.

Constitution of parish meetings and establishment of parish councils.

    (*a*) shall, if the parish meeting of a rural parish having a population of one hundred or upwards so resolve, provide for establishing a parish council in the parish, and may, with the consent of the parish meeting of any rural parish having a population of less than one hundred, provide for establishing a parish council in the parish; and

    (*b*) may provide for grouping a parish with some neighbouring parish or parishes under a common parish council, but with a separate parish meeting for every parish so grouped, so, however, that no parish shall be grouped without the consent of the parish meeting for that parish.

INDEX